For Scott & Elizabeth —
the best is yet to come!

Don
Dec 4, 04

Deep Calls to Deep

Deep Calls to Deep

HOW CHRIST EMPOWERS LIVES OF SERVICE

Donald A. Webb

©1998 by Donald A. Webb

Volunteers of America

Published by
Volunteers of America, Inc.
110 South Union Street
Alexandria, VA 22314
1-800-899-0089
www.voa.org

Book and cover design: John Costa, New Orleans
Editorial consultant: A.M. Smith & Company, New Orleans

ISBN: 1-885287-02-X

Printed in the United States of America

2nd Edition

Deep calls to deep
in the roar of thy cataracts,
and all thy waves, all thy breakers,
pass over me.

The Lord makes his unfailing love
shine forth
alike by day and night;
his praise on my lips is a prayer
to the God of my life.

Psalm 42:7-8

For Renee

OVER FIFTY YEARS,
BEST SHIPMATE,
OFTEN ON DEEP WATERS.

Acknowledgements

For his affirmation from the beginning, I want to thank Chuck Gould, president of Volunteers of America; for the gentle but insistent urging of Dianna Kunz, and of my old friend and mentor Everett Tilson; for the unfailing support of Chuck Meehan, himself a stalwart servant; and for his boundless patience and skill, my editor Arthur Smith.

Contents

Prologue: To a good voyage!	3
Chapter 1: The call in the deep	5
Chapter 2: The lifting life	11
Chapter 3: As life comes to us, and we come to life!	20
Chapter 4: To serve by the Christing of our eyes	28
Chapter 5: Our ears open, and we speak plain	36
Chapter 6: Deeper than our hearts	44
Chapter 7: To serve by enabling prayer	53
Chapter 8: God's detours	60
Chapter 9: A hard question yields to the great vocation	68
Chapter 10: Getting the message, at last	78
Chapter 11: How our daily grind becomes daily grace	88
Chapter 12: The age of the spirit	96
Chapter 13: The spirit's compass-course	104
Chapter 14: The vision fulfilled	114
Epilogue: By the light of a good sunset	121

Deep Calls to Deep

Prologue: to a good voyage!

By way of introduction, I am a former sea captain who became a pastor; a former Brit who became an American; a former scholar seduced into administration; a former college president who wanted to be a servant. So I joined the board of a group devoted to helping people, the Volunteers of America; and swiftly their work astonished this newcomer.

In Shreveport, Louisiana where I live, Volunteers of America's commissioned ministers, staff and volunteers provide amazingly varied services: pregnancy counseling and adoption facilities; homes and community help for people with developmental disabilities and mental illness. They offer what may be this region's preeminent agency for salvaging and enabling lives, "The Lighthouse," whose range of programs elicit in young people, pre-school to after-school, the desire and means to education, self-confidence and competence, and furnish for all ages training for jobs, parenting, leadership. Whatever it takes to release human potential.

And soon there was a task for me, daunting but exhilarating. Volunteers of America is a church, founded to embody Christ's servant ministry. What they do, they do well. Yet there's a hunger for a deeper spiritual reality. So they asked me to explore with them the deep life of the spirit, and its empowerment for service. This quest in God's commissioning Word is my grateful offering.

But surely this is the search of every believer? Our time and society desperately need Good Samaritans. Perhaps other servant-pilgrims will use this resource, to stimulate discussion, to find commitment. I do hope so. Each chapter locates in a Word of God, by which we may so experience grace that we ourselves are empowered to serve. Each is informed by the spirit and caring ministry of Jesus of Nazareth. I have also learned much from Maud and Ballington Booth who founded this servant church called Volunteers of America.

PROLOGUE • TO A GOOD VOYAGE!

I come at the task out of my own pilgrimage and understandings. As a student of scripture who was formerly a sailor of seas, I respond especially to Biblical accounts of happenings on deep waters, symbols of profound spiritual life. I come to test my own deep-sea experiences as such pointers. My hope is that these scriptural soundings may salt our search in the sense of Matthew 5:13, where Jesus, having lifted up those who shall obtain mercy, see God, and be called sons, then commissions his followers "salt of the earth."

"Soundings" measure sea-depths: although God's grace is fathomless, we can plumb deep enough to experience the power we need for a life of service. And "soundings" also "sound forth." Here are declarations of our gratitude for grace received, and joy in living it out. So may this book be a vessel that takes us out into the deep things of God to discover who we are and what our task is.

For me, the heart of Christian faith is this: By grace, living in Christ shapes like a cross. As we stretch our arms wide like his to serve others, he leads us to the depth of God's compassion. And our whole being surges to a lifting life.

Chapter 1: The call in the deep

From John 21:

> *Simon Peter said to them, "I'm going fishing." "We'll go with you." But that night they caught nothing. Just as day was breaking, Jesus stood on the beach…He called to them, "Cast on the right side of the boat." Now they weren't able to haul in, for the quantity of fish. "It's the Lord!" When Simon Peter heard that, he sprang into the sea. The other disciples came in the boat, dragging the net full of fish…When they got on land, they saw a charcoal fire there, with fish lying on it, and bread…Jesus said to them, "Come and have breakfast…"*
>
> *When they had finished, Jesus said to Simon Peter, "Simon, son of John, do you love me more than these?" He said to him, "Yes, Lord; you know that I love you." He said to him, "Feed my lambs." A second time he said to him, "Simon, son of John, do you love me?" He said to him, "Yes, Lord; you know that I love you." He said to him, "Tend my sheep." He said to him a third time, "Simon, son of John, do you love me?" Peter was grieved because he said to him the third time, "Do you love me?" And he said to him, "Lord, you know everything; you know that I love you." Jesus said to him, "Feed my sheep."*

The question is: "Do you really want to serve?" Simon decided beside the sea.

We meet him for the first time on a beach. His brother Andrew is running along the shore, calling Simon from his boat. Andrew had met a man who'd change everything. For some reason, Simon does come ashore, and meets Jesus of Nazareth. To help Simon discover his true self, Jesus sends him back out on the deep…three times.

Luke 5:3-8 tells us of the first time. Jesus gets into Simon's boat. "Put out into deep water and let down your nets." Simon argues, "We were hard at it all night and caught nothing…but if you say, I will." They make a haul that split the nets and Simon falls to the deck on his knees: "Leave me, Lord," he says, "I'm a sinner."

Is that where self-discovery begins? As Genesis says, we are made of "dust of the earth." Of course, we have that other side of us, which Genesis calls "the image of God." But it's usually our dirt that rises to the top. Self-understanding begins with our facing up to it, perhaps like Simon, on our knees.

When we do, Christ will have taken us on our first voyage of self-discovery.

Simon's second voyage is related in Matthew 22. Jesus tells the disciples to set sail while he goes to pray. Soon the boat is battling head winds and a rough sea. They're in grave danger, even the sailors sure they'll drown. Jesus comes to them, walking on the water. They think it's a ghost, but he calls, "Take heart, it's I. Don't be afraid." Simon shouts, "Lord, if it is you, tell me to come to you over the water." "Come!" Simon steps on the sea, and walks toward him.

Again, they had embarked because Jesus sent them. And the storm breaks. You might think if you do what God wants, you wouldn't get storms in your life. But right where you sit, God's Word can precipitate storms in your mind and soul. It's what you do next that can lift you to a new crest! The small boat of their existence is almost swamped, when he comes — in a totally unexpected way. (This is how Jesus comes to us, in ways we shouldn't presume). "Take heart, it's I."

Simon impulsively wants to leap before he looks. That may be wiser than looking so long, you never do make the leap of faith. The fact is Simon is moving in his deep-water discovery of himself. Once you begin to know authentic life, it draws you trembling forward. Aware now that he is a mixture of earth and divinity, he must find out if he can live by the godly side of him. "Come," says Jesus, in that characteristic response to eager faith. He doesn't promise Simon can do it easily, but "Come!" And that's enough. Pushing the boat from under him, Simon steps on the sea.

Try it. All of us are made in the image of God. We don't have to live a dust-of-the earth way. True, Simon soon feels the terror of wind and waves, and down he goes. Mostly our ventures of faith are brief; as soon as I take my eyes off God, that's me, too!

He cries for help, not easy for a proud man, and soon he's in the boat beside Jesus. The rest are silent, as they should be. They haven't even got their feet wet because their eyes were on their difficulties, instead of on their Christ. The storm is over and Simon has discovered that living God's way is possible, if one dares.

Simon has one more voyage ahead before he is a rock and a servant.

It's just before dawn on the gray Sea of Tiberias. In the boat out in the haze, the men are tired and desolate. Jesus, of whom they had hoped so much, had been crucified on Calvary. What's life for now? They might as well return to the old ways of living, before the great hope he had lit in their minds. Indeed, it was Simon, perhaps from some fathomless sense in him, who suggested this voyage. They've sailed all night in desultory fashion, catching nothing. It's almost light. Should they give up now and go home? What's the point?

They drift near the beach. Then they see a man, hear his voice across the water. "It's the Lord!" Everyone's head comes up and Simon leaps overboard, half swims, half runs to shore.

Many of us have been out on that first voyage to learn that though we're divinity and dirt, we act mostly out of the dirt. We felt the benediction of shame and are thereby able to move realistically into a healing future. Some have gone deeper, daring to live through moments of total trust, venturing to think God's way.

And to those who long most earnestly for the lifting life that lasts forever, comes a moment of hearing the truth like daybreak in the heart: a moment of turning, of knowing! And landward, as you look, it's light!

There are things ordinary language just cannot express. Suppose I ask you to describe what you feel about your mother. How easy would that be? Think back down your years with her, from a baby, through childhood and the teenages, how she felt about you, what she meant to you, the countless words and acts between you. Now put all that into just a few words, into the prosaic bread-and-butter words which are all we have? It can't be done.

But when people of faith try to say what the lifting life means, though it may also come out as new attitudes to people, or released potential, or love, or joy, always at the crux of it is the sense of Christ's living presence. That's what the Gospel tries to convey. There's been a sea-change! From the experience in your deep, you come to this new relationship, standing on firm ground in your life, sun shining all round. The deep is behind you — though you may go back from time to time for other self-discovery, but without fear. You know at the deepest in you Christ is here! The sense of his presence is near as breathing, closer than hands and feet; not only read about in the Bible, or hoped for when we pray; not just witnessed in history or the testimony of others: the sense of Christ's living presence has become the main reality of life.

And what is Christ saying? He asks, how much do you love? The crucial question is not about creeds or denominations but, "**Do** you love? Do **you** love? Do you **love**?" And most marvelously, as it's asked of the deepest humanity in us we can say, "Yes, Lord!"

Then Christ tells us how to use this love: "Feed my lambs." The love is only for sharing: "Tend my sheep." Only for people and their needs: "Feed my sheep." He says to us, "If you want to love and serve me, do it through your fellow human beings. I don't need it. They do." And God has sent us into the deepest part of our being, to find our best self, and know gratefully this wonder in our deep. Yes!

In this so difficult time, when much of what we value seems drifting away, we discover the lifting life and commit to its service, helping people. We will continue to struggle, in God's grace, for clearer understanding, and a clearer way of speaking to our own hearts and our own time; meanwhile, until those fresh ways disclose themselves, we help make life less inhumane. The way forward is here: "Feed my sheep." And we are servants.

As I prepared the above, I was very moved to have open beside my writing pad the personal New Testament (King James version) of Ballington Booth, who with his wife Maud founded Volunteers of America. In his beautiful handwriting, interspersed in its pages, are his notes for the sermons he preached across America. And from the first ("The Touch of Compassion") to the last (on the difficulties God permits "to bring His servants to real and aggressive service") the commission "feed my lambs" is implicit, clear, and primary. For readers unacquainted with the great story of what Ballington Booth in his New Testament often refers to as "V of A," I commend Dr. Herbert A. Wisbey's *Era of the Founders*. The founders understood — stood under, indeed! — their Lord's priority of compassionate servanthood. Hear Maud Booth identify the key to her pioneering prison ministry: "What they needed from my lips was…from Christ's dear heart of love." Wisbey writes, it's "hard to believe, in this cynical age, that a woman could so touch an audience of convicted criminals …that fifty would brave the jeers…of their fellow prisoners…stand up and signify publicly their desire to lead a new life."

Wisbey describes the incident which brought Maud Booth to her great life's work among the men and women in America's prisons:

> *The postman had dumped a large bag of mail on Mrs. Booth's makeshift desk…One letter caused her to spring up and hurry over to her husband. It was a crudely written appeal from a prisoner in Sing Sing Prison asking her to consider the problems of the men behind bars and begging her to visit them. On the back was a note from Warden Omar V. Sage extending an official invitation to visit the prison and address the men.*

She went, of course. And over the next 52 years devoted a considerable part of her life to working directly with the prisoners, both while they were incarcerated and after their release. She helped the convicts' families and she became their advocates before the general public. Yet, as she said, her compassion was not "that foolish, unbalanced ardor of sentiment that looks upon all criminals as much wronged unfortunates who are to be pitied not blamed for their condition." Indeed, she had a keen sense of horror for crime, wrong, and sin. But as she put it:

If Christ came to seek and save the lost, if Christ spoke of heaven to the thief on Calvary, if He loves and offers hope to the hopeless, we ought to be able lovingly and tenderly to banish the past from our memory, pointing to the future with all it can hold for them if they will but make use of Christ's good offer of forgiveness, cleansing and saving power. Christ loves the sinner though he loathes the sin that has stained and spoiled his life.

One of the prisoners remembers her saying:

I don't come here to prevent you from paying the just penalty of your crimes; take your medicine like men. You know what is right, do it now. When you have paid the penalty, I will help you. I will nurse you back to health. I will get you work. Above all, I will trust you, and it depends upon you whether I keep on doing so or not. Mind, I will help you over the rough places, but I will not carry you..."

And for her husband Ballington, the same priority: "Christianity to be a power must be an all round blessing and gain — must not affect the mind and spirit only but the body and physical surroundings. There must not merely be the feeding of the soul with bread of life but the *feeding of the body* with the physical bread. Again, "the poor man needed a coat that he might come to hear of the Gospel, the invalid child...a nurse that it might be restored to health, to attend God's house, the famishing one...cold water and the kindly touch of the Samaritan that he might live". He urges servants in Christ to have "tenderness of touch". And in the center of his New Testament, alongside his underlined Luke 7:22, *"Tell John what things ye have seen and heard,"* is his hand-written note, "He came to give men a second chance!"

Feed my lambs.

Chapter 2: The lifting life

From Mark 5:

> *They came to the other side of the sea, to the country of the Gerasenes. And when (Jesus) had come out of the boat, there met him out of the tombs a man with an unclean spirit, who lived among the tombs; and no one could bind him any more, even with a chain; for he had often been bound with fetters and chains, but the chains he wrenched apart, and the fetters he broke in pieces; and no one had the strength to subdue him. Night and day among the tombs and on the mountains he was always crying out, and bruising himself with stones...Jesus asked him, "What is your name?" He replied, "My name is Legion; for we are many." And he begged him eagerly not to send them out of the country. Now a great herd of swine was feeding there on the hillside; and they begged him, "Send us to the swine, let us enter them." So he gave them leave. And the unclean spirits came out, and entered the swine; and the herd, numbering about two thousand, rushed down the steep bank into the sea, and were drowned in the sea.*
>
> *The herdsmen fled, and told it in the city and in the country. And people came to see what it was that had happened. And they came to Jesus, and saw the demoniac sitting there, clothed in his right mind, the man who had had the legion; and they were afraid...And as (Jesus) was getting into the boat, the man who had been possessed with demons begged him that he might be with him.*

An old sea memory has floated up. And I wonder why now?

Imagine a June day off the English coast. His Majesty's Ship *Barbastel* was fixing the positions of deep water buoys, and inspecting their hardware on the ocean bottom. I was "Jimmy-the-One," her Executive Officer at the ripe age of 22. On this occasion, Captain Embleton was on leave, so I was in charge.

The routine was for our diver to go down and survey the anchors and chains while I checked surface position with instruments. This time the diver had found the shackles down there suspect and questioned whether to replace them. It was a big job. With Jimmy-the-One bravado — considering I'd never been on the bottom of the sea before — I decided to inspect the moorings in person. So on that bright June day, two sailors rowed me and the diver out to the troublesome buoy.

You've never put on a diving suit? Not scuba stuff but deep-sea equipment, complete with Charlie Chaplin lead-weighted boots? It's like being entombed in rubber. It took 20 minutes to stuff me into the thing.

The two sailors started turning the pump handles. I'd depend on them for the rubbery-smelling air I was getting. I took a last look round. All I could see was distorted, the glass so thick it goggled the vision. But I did see the diver's huge eye through my window, winking at me.

On our primitive intercom he gave me friendly tips on what to do down there. But I was busy being nonchalant, as Royal Navy Officers do. He put a rope in my hand: "It's your lifeline," he mouthed, "If you need me, shout on the intercom and I'll come down." I shouted back, "No problem!"

Feeling with my boot for the rung below, I climbed down, the suit cold against my legs, waist, and chest. Then bright bubbles swirled in front of my eyes. Feeling further with the boot, I was out of rungs, just deep water below. I let go the ladder. The sea closed over and I sank. The water got dark blue, blue-black, black, pitch black. When the tide runs swift off that coast, all the muck of the bottom swirls up. Still, I wasn't prepared for the darkness. It shook me.

So did the noise: loud hissings, bubblings, swishings from who knows what. I couldn't hear the diver, up topside.

And as soon as I let go the ladder, I started to rotate. I had no idea how to stop. Until after what seemed endless spiraling down through black noise, I felt my boots squish into the ooze on the bottom of the sea. I clung to that rope.

To my dismay, I couldn't get my balance. My boots heavy in the mud, a strong tide pushing at my back, I thrashed about trying to get upright — knowing if I lifted one foot, I'd fall on my face.

And in spiraling down, I had lost direction. Which way were the anchors? And what was out there looming in the dark? I swear eels were slithering around my legs. Should I call the diver? But the crew would snigger that the Exec got chicken first time he went deep. No, I'd stick it out awhile, pretend I'd done the job, then go up.

So I clung to the rope, struggling to get upright. But I couldn't cope with the pressure, couldn't walk, see, hear the diver, couldn't much longer keep from falling forward. And I was terrified of going down into that mud. Call! But what would they say?

Then suddenly a fierce thrust of pressure sent me stumbling forward, flailing with both arms to keep from falling. I'd let go the lifeline! I grabbed in the darkness, but at a shadow, and it was gone. Lashing desperately about, I couldn't stop falling forward into the mud. My helmet buried in it. I knew I would never get up. The air supply would foul under the slime and I would suffocate on the bottom of the sea.

I was desperate to calm myself but the mud was like a bog. My helmet was too heavy to lift. The sweat ran in my eyes. Try again! But the helmet sucked deeper as I wrestled. Christ, this is awful!

And then I felt a hand touching my back. The diver had come down! He grasped my shoulders, and lifted, and helped me struggle to my feet as I held on to him. Gave me a "thumbs up:" He had surely been through this. I could even hear his voice, now, as I peered hard through the glass and watched him speak. He showed me how to stand against the tide.

The confusion began clearing a bit. Gradually he let go and showed me where the lifeline was. I took it, trying to control myself. He led me through the muck to the moorings. They were there, all right: anchors well-set, rusty chains, shackles that had to be removed. I should have seen them myself. He showed me how he walked upright, and before long had me working with him somewhat, clearing the chains, freeing the shackles, starting the job I was supposed to do.

But as I said why this memory now?

Perhaps that long-ago struggle on the bottom of the sea rises up now because I'm more ready to deal with it now — and need its meaning, now! Could it be a kind of symbol of a more general human possibility? Of a journey down into the depth of things? Of finding ourselves graciously connecting with a reality that lifts us to the heights of life, empowering our hands and beings to serve our fellows? Could my ordeal be like our human struggle?

Take those weighted Frankenstein boots. We were meant to run clean through life with grace and beauty, surrounded, as Scripture says (Heb. 12:1), "by so great a cloud of witnesses." But we're weighed down by flaws of character and the wrongs we do.

And isn't there a thick distorting glass between you and all you perceive? Every person and relationship, every question, you look at from your own viewpoint. Even Paul, who tried hard to see faithfully, knew that the best we do is look "through a glass, darkly" (1 Cor. 13:12).

What do you hear in your life? Incessant noise. The pitchman's voice persuading, the politician's babel, the rustle of money. Somewhere in the world's racket, a voice full of grace and truth does speak. But it's lost in the din. As in a running tide, pressures work on our appetites and ambitions. Disorientation is obvious the moment you hear people speak of their beliefs or principles, and then look at how they get ahead. I'm talking about me. And you, too, perhaps? And how we modern people dread going down into the earth, don't we? Into the grave?

Or consider this sad anomaly. The average 24 hours here are more violent than almost anywhere not at war; with more criminals and victims, more incarcerated or executed, more drug abuse, child abuse, wife abuse. Moral values deteriorated every time you take in the news or a movie. Yet we are a religious nation. The percentage of Americans attending worship is higher than in Britain, Italy, France, or most Western countries. Our society displays a sad antithesis: corroded, yet very pious.

Or consider happiness. Ours is a fun-seeking generation, among the most pleasure-bent in history. Whatever else our work and wages are for they must provide leisure and means enough for lots of amusement. So those who play the games we watch or the guitars we hear are paid far more than the life-and-death people of our land. Even in church, it's "don't be too tough, Rev. Start with a joke, y'hear — plenty of warm stories. Be upbeat — celebrate!" We insist on our children having a good time, including their education, "No drudgery, now: make it fun. Beguile them into getting it." So no tough discipline, either; in school life, T.V. life, sex life, anything.

At some level, fun-philosophy may work. Until real life — or death — hits the marriage or the family. It's pretty thin stuff then. Fear, loneliness, or depression are daily tormentors for innumerable folk, or mental and emotional problems fester. Suicide, even by the young, is far from rare.

We are devout, but demoralized; bent on enjoying ourselves, yet many are so unhappy. Surely one has to wonder if religion has become superficial, and doesn't lift life any more? Perhaps we don't respond to God deeply enough? And could this be why, at this precise time in our history, the two main entities able and expected to lift the desperately down are retreating from the front line of service? The government, pressed by voters, increasingly turns from meeting people's needs; and the churches, too, face inward, their eggs in the Sunday basket of togetherness and celebration. Despair spirals.

What might happen if we open ourselves deeply to the life force of God speaking in us and let the Holy Spirit break through? Life might lift: body, soul, and mind empowered to serve!

I am reminded of another seafarer, Captain John Newton. He was born in 1725 to a brutal situation. At 11 he went, probably impressed, into naval service. The years of his harsh nurture included flogging for desertion, harrowing escapes, even slavery under brutal masters. Faithless, without hope and at times suicidal, he grappled his way up to command a ship. He transported slaves.

But as a child, he had learned the love of God from his mother. Later it also came to him in a sweet girl, his future wife, Mary Catlett. And a chance exposure (chance?) caused him to avidly read Thomas à Kempis, the English mystic.

And then there happened what he called his "Great Deliverance." Voyaging home, he came near to drowning in a waterlogged vessel. Inexplicably, he was brought safely through. It was his culminating experience in the deep, and he became a man of Christ, his best service writing words of life that lift:

> *Amazing grace! How sweet the sound*
> *That saved a wretch like me!*
> *I once was lost, but now am found;*
> *Was blind, but now I see.*
> *Through many dangers, toils and snares*
> *I have already come;*
> *'Tis grace hath brought me safe thus far,*
> *And grace will lead me home.*

Time and again, the Scriptures draw us to this level of connection with God. "The inward mind and heart are deep," (Ps. 64:6), "the mind like deep water" (Proverbs 20). "By (God's) knowledge, the depths break forth" say Proverbs 3:20; and Genesis 49:25 proclaims "the blessings of the deep." Job affirms "(God) brings deep darkness to light" (Job 21:22). In Psalm 92:5, the people of faith declare, "How great are thy works, O God: thy thoughts are very deep." God speaks to us, as the words of Psalm 42:7 echo in us, "deep to deep!"

Consider the birth of Methodism, where, through The Salvation Army, Volunteers of America has its roots. On May 24, 1738, John Wesley went to worship in St. Paul's Cathedral. The choir sang Psalm 13, *Out of the Deep Have I Called unto Thee: O God, Hear My Voice.* It was, he said, as if his own soul were pleading with God. That evening, Wesley was drawn to a meeting of people seeking faith. There, while a man was describing the change which God works in the heart through faith in Christ, he felt his own heart strangely warmed. He trusted in Christ, Christ alone, for salvation, assured that

Christ had taken away his sins and had saved him.

This is what happens when "deep calls to deep." That warmth in John Wesley's heart caught fire in him; then in others, and others, across the country, across the sea. And though a thin, shy, small man, plagued by bad health, for his remaining years he rode on horseback the length and breadth of Britain, preaching more than 42,000 sermons, often to crowds goaded to throw abuse, stones, and mud. And in spite of all they did to him, his heart was full of love for them, his eyes with tears, and his mouth with argument. Wesley could not have imagined such a re-created life before his experience in the deep at St. Paul's.

Not that it was a sudden conversion. There had been years of search and struggle to respond to God's tug. Years before, in Oxford, with his brother Charles and other Anglican priests, he was distressed that theirs was a decaying and irrelevant church. They had determined to take Christ utterly seriously in daily life, to be *methodical* about their faith. They met each morning for prayer, fasted every Wednesday and Friday, and after their studies and work, helped the prisoners in the jails and the poor in the slums. Then John became a missionary in America. Meanwhile his fellows continued trying to spread across England their methodical and punctilious piety.

But though these "Methodists" strove hard, they failed to become vital Christians. And little changed in the English church. John, knowing no success abroad, returned troubled. Taking one's religion seriously wasn't enough. Yet he had learned something. On the dangerous voyage over the deeps of the Atlantic, a hurricane terrified all aboard — except a group of Moravian Christians, in whom Wesley saw a kind of faith he didn't have.

And then it happened to him: that service in St. Paul's. And he was hurled into a renewed life and a refreshed ministry and a revived church.

My own quick personal index to this revolution are two books, side by side on my library shelf, written 21 years apart yet different as chalk from cheese. One is Henry Fielding's *Tom Jones* (1720), funny, outrageous, agonizing; a hit movie was made of it in 1963. The other is

John Wesley's *Sermons*, searching, liberating, transforming, but rarely opened today, and then only briefly by Methodist seminarians.

Fielding's comic genius was to trick his readers. His depraved, hilarious characters tickled them, and then showed them they were laughing at themselves. The well-to-do, typified by the overfed Squire Western, lived for their pleasures, using their captive poor, women and men, to satisfy their appetites. And the poor — depicted as degraded, filthy, dishonest beasts — drowned themselves in cheap gin.

The Church, chill and irrelevant, was part of this decaying mess. It tranquilized both the Squire Westerns by glorifying them and their country, and the poor, by keeping them docile here on the promise of a crown hereafter. It *is* funny. But it breaks your heart. And though there may be some writer's exaggeration, historians generally tend to confirm it.

Yet 21 years later John Wesley was able to describe his congregations as honest, sober, and upright, ready to help others with their time and money, wanting to obey God's law, and living peaceably with all. There may be some preacherly exaggeration, but certainly between 1720 and 1741, something radically changed the society of *Tom Jones* into the transformed people of Wesley's *Sermons*. Indeed, France's Elie Halevy (1870 - 1937) in *A History of the English People In the 19th Century* and the modern English historian E.P. Thompson in *The Rise of the Working Class in England* assert it was the creation of Methodism that prevented a "French Revolution" in Britain. Across the Channel the same inhumane conditions had long prevailed: the well-off squeezed the life out of the poor until they could stand it no longer. The result was slaughter. Whereas in England newborn Christ-people, rich and poor, discovered they could reform, spread education, enable a humane life for all, politically, economically and socially. They established schools, cared for the sick and imprisoned, battled slavery, and strove for world peace. They set, lived, and insisted on high moral values — and committed their lives to servanthood.

To you who would also serve: it is in contexts like these that we read Mark 5 with personal hope. A demented outcast, forced from home, lives out among the tombs, writhing. (There's a terrifying journey into the depths!) But Christ comes to meet him, the God of health in Christ enabling the man to talk about his demons, so many and so brutal he calls them "Legion!" He and Jesus look at each other, and he responds to the love of God in Christ, to the healing and joy, until he's still, arms quiet, knowing, in the rushing away of the swine, that his devils are gone. He's clear now.

And listen. The healed man wants to go with Christ, and join him in his life of service.

Chapter 3: As Life comes to us, and we come to life!

From John, chapter 4:

(Jesus) left Judea and departed again to Galilee. He had to pass through Samaria. So he came to a city of Samaria, called Sychar, near to the field that Jacob gave to his son Joseph. Jacob's well was there, and so Jesus, wearied as he was with his journey, sat down beside the well. It was about the sixth hour.

There came a woman of Samaria to draw water. Jesus said to her, "Give me a drink." For his disciples had gone away into the city to buy food. The Samaritan woman said to him, "How is it that you, a Jew, ask a drink of me, a woman of Samaria?" For Jews have no dealings with Samaritans. Jesus answered her, "If you knew the gift of God, and who it is that is saying to you, 'Give me a drink,' you would have asked him, and he would have given you living water." The woman said to him, "Sir, you have nothing to draw with, and the well is deep: where do you get that living water?" ...Jesus said to her, "Whoever drinks of the water that I shall give him will never thirst, (it) will become in him a spring of water, welling up to eternal life." " — Sir, give me this water, that I may not thirst..." Jesus said to her, "Go, call your husband." "...I have no husband." "You are right...for you have had five husbands, and he whom you now have is not your husband." The woman said to him, "Sir, I perceive that you are a prophet. Our fathers worshipped on this mountain, and you say that in Jerusalem is where men ought to worship." "Woman, believe me...the hour is coming, and now is, when true worshippers will worship the Father in spirit and in truth..." The woman said, "I know that the Messiah is coming, and when he comes, he will show us all things." Jesus said to her, "I who speak to you am he."

...So the woman left her water jar, went away into the city, and said to the people, "Come see a man who told me all that I ever did. Can this be the Christ?" They went out of the city and were coming to him.

However our days are spent, something is miserably amiss if we do not from time to time drink at the deep wells of sacredness. But if we do, life is lifted — into Life!

If our days are to be spent in helping people, this event in John's Gospel draws us to a deep well of empowerment. Even more: As we find that God's family becomes our family, it's the whole human family we serve.

But let's pause a moment and ask why "deep wells?"

In the Bible, deep water is often where people discover God. Right at the beginning in Genesis, as people emerge from what they call "the darkness…upon the face of the deep," they sense they're not just animals, but created by a loving God. And as they look out upon their world, the ocean pounding into shore so resembles their own wave-like inner impulses, always threatening to engulf them, they see it as terrifying, like the turbulence inside them. No wonder they come to believe it is God who holds back both the fearful ocean and our inner selves from submerging us. In the symbol of the sea, early people called to faith, discovered how vulnerable we are, and how strong God is.

Noah, in the immense waters flooding the earth, knew our radical choice. We must live God's way, or be overwhelmed. A key self-understanding of God's people came when they fled slavery in Egypt, with only the Red Sea between them and their future. God opened the sea, led them through and showed them what they were chosen for. Having crossed dry-shod, they came to 12 wells; they decided to encamp there. And the Lord made a covenant with them. It's not only water that God's people draw from deep wells.

Or when we hear Psalm 42:7, in which "deep calls to deep," may we sense God's Spirit breaking through to our human spirit! And when the Spirit of God speaks deep within us, life will never be the same. Or as Psalm 107 declares, "They that go down to the sea in ships, that do their business in great waters, these see the works of the Lord, and his wonders in the deep."

In the fullness of time, Jesus came, "nurtured in the water of a womb." Grown to manhood, he went down into the Jordan for baptism, for total self-awareness, "This is my beloved Son." He knew then what he must do. Often, throughout the Gospels, Jesus is "on the sea," or "beside the sea," teaching or performing miracles, all piercing our dullness to reveal how his Life comes into our lives.

And he created his church — a ship! Where the people worship is called "the Nave," as in "navy," from "navis," a ship. When a church is truly being the Church, it's that divine vessel which takes its people out into profound truths, to discover who God is, who we are, and the quality of life of the Servant.

So we are not surprised that at deep wells, significant things happen. Jesus meets this Samaritan woman at Jacob's well. This is where Judeo-Christian faith had its beginnings. It is described in such detail in Genesis 29:1-10, it may have burrowed deep into faith's memory. So though we may not hear it consciously, now from the Gospel comes a profound echo of our spiritual dawn, far deeper than mere recollection, down at the very roots of our beliefs. As we approach the account of Jesus at Jacob's Well, there's a stirring of the waters of our soul.

And if humanity is indeed one family and God's family, it's not surprising either that many other cultures have symbolic wells, too. There is the Well of Knowledge in Norse mythology, where the ash-tree Yggrasil, supporting the universe, sends its roots. The Mayans had their Well of Sacrifice, the Sacred Cenote. Even we skeptical moderns have our "wishing wells."

Perhaps depth psychology can help us here. It visualizes our psyche as three strata. Near the surface is our "conscious" mind, containing all we're aware of. Below, a much thicker stratum, is our "personal unconscious," containing those psychic materials of a personal nature which are not raised to consciousness, not easily identified, but crucially shaping our attitudes and actions. Helpful, loving and creative influences may originate and nurture there, but so may unhealthy, distorting, even destructive forces, the complexes, repressions, dark fixations, and strange compulsions which ruin happiness.

But the deepest stratum is our "collective unconscious," a vast storehouse of ancient experience and patterns of humanness. They are sensed rather than known, common to all across the world. In the collective unconscious the idea of a deep well, or of deep water anywhere, in the ocean, in lakes, in rivers, crosses cultures and religions.

This way of understanding our psyche can help us as we seek the lifting life of service to the human family. Deep within each of us, in our soul — the soul and the "unconscious" are different ways of talking about what's most profound in us — are those spiritual materials of a personal nature, and deepest of all in our souls is that common human spirit which makes us one humanity, children of the one God. Our spirit is the storehouse of those patterns and understandings that the Creator has been sharing and nurturing deep within us since we were created in his image.

We repsond out of this common spiritual storehouse then, when we meet Jesus at Jacob's well.

I ask you to imagine this encounter in the desert. It's midday, the sun scorching your skin, your mouth dry as the sand. From where you are beside the well you can see the heat shimmering. Shade your eyes, and look into the far distance. You can make out a cloud of dust, miles away, barely moving.

Time passes. The dust is closer now. You can see men walking slowly. At last they come to where you are, and go on. Except one man. He stops and sits down at the well, tiredness in every muscle, his beard streaked with dust. If he were to lean over the well, his hot skin would feel its freshness rising, for deep down in the earth it reaches cold water. But he only leans back against the well. Everything is quiet.

In a sense, there's no way to avoid this scene. It must happen. Verse 4 reads, "(Jesus) had to pass through Samaria." Why did he "have" to? The road from Galilee went around Samaria. But Jesus had to pass through, Scripture says. Perhaps because what needs to happen won't happen if he goes another way? Samaria was a Gentile country: our kind of country. Maybe he has to go through so you and I can hear

God's Word to us? And grasp how to live; maybe it's for our sake he has to go through?

Verse 5: "So he came to a city called Sychar...Jacob's well was there." So it's to be a *kairos* meeting! *Kairos* is when our spirit opens profoundly to the inbursting Spirit of God; when what is of earth uncloses to receive what is of heaven, like a fist unclenching to accept a caress, or a bud outspreading to the sun. It's a Michelangelo moment. You recall the Sistine Chapel ceiling where God's finger stretches to humankind, and ours reaches back, about to touch: *kairos*! Mark 1:14,15 proclaims, "Jesus came...announcing that...the *kairos* is fully here, the reign of God." In Paul's letter to the Ephesians 1:9,10, "(God) has made known to us the... fulfillment of the *kairos*." It's the moment you realize Jesus of Nazareth is your Christ. We're to meet Jesus of Nazareth at Jacob's well. It's that time.

"And Jesus," (verse 6) "wearied as he was...sat down beside the well." Worn out! There isn't a word here that doesn't draw us to the encounter! Because John calls Jesus "Lord," and he knows his Ten Commandments as well as you do: you don't call anyone "Lord" but God. God is here, John is saying, slumped against a well, bringing you hard to the fact that Christ bears no signs of who he is, is not surrounded by angels, has no lighted halo you see in paintings, or any material evidence you're in God's presence. Only as you open your being to him in this *kairos* moment will you know him.

"It was about the sixth hour." That is, about noon, the moment when the sun is right overhead, with no shadows. If you're ever going to see things as they really are, it's now. If ever you're going to let in the affirming truth, it's now. It's not clock time or chronos time, but *kairos* time, unlocking time, throwing-open time, inbreaking time, lifting time. Time for encounter with Christ!

The encounter begins in (verse 7). "There came a woman of Samaria to draw water." There are two things wrong with her. First, she's a woman. Women in that day were not considered persons as men are persons, they were assets, though above the cows and sheep. Second, she's a Samaritan, and in that context, disgusting — of a race little better than goats. That's why the road from Judea went *round* Samaria, not *through* it. Going through would make one feel dirty. John makes us look at the tragedy of how human beings look down on other human beings. And it's not just that we're what the Bible calls "sinful," but that being so, we still want self-esteem, and the easiest way to get it is to look down on someone else. He who looks down feels superior: it's a delusion of self-worth. "Give me a drink?" Jesus asks. It's a *kairos* question!

I want to pause here and note two facts in the history of Volunteers of America which, since I learned them, have made me grateful and inspired. In 1896, long before most of Western culture, the original Constitution devised by Maud and Ballington Booth affirmed: "It is to be distinctly understood that the Volunteers of America recognize woman as man's equal." As you follow John's account of Jesus speaking to the Samaritan woman, you suspect that the Booths, too, responded to Christ at a deep well of sacredness! Again, in 1934, when news began to come in of the Nazis' atrocities against the Jews, in America and the democracies generally the response was mainly silence; perhaps an occasional murmur of indignation, but no action. The Volunteers of America spoke out vehemently in a strong editorial in the March 1934 *Volunteer's Gazette*: "Christianity Aroused by Persecution in Germany." Again, are here the Booths and their colleagues responding to Christ at a deep well of sacredness?

Jesus asks this Samaritan woman for a drink. And she must ask: "How can you ask a Samaritan for help?"

Often, as you read the Bible, some phrase goes right to your heart, and it hurts. Jesus' reply is a painful one for me: "If only you knew," he says. When I was young, and at Cambridge and knew it all, my mother, who had not been to college, sometimes would try to share with me about her faith, and I'd brush her off with, "Come on, Mom: drop it." She'd say, sort of helplessly, "If only you knew…" Well, it took many years to come home to me; and now she's not here for us to share. Sad words, then for many folk, perhaps?

"If only you knew," Jesus says, "You would ask him, and he would give you living water." The Gospel is bringing us close now to what this is all about — to what life is all about! What is "living water"? Jesus is speaking of a quality of life that runs and dances and sparkles! It's being gloriously attuned to God's love: it's releasing to God's "Yes!" It's *kairos*! It's health and meaning and joy! He's inviting you to compassionate service alongside him! And he calls it "living water." Are you open to it?

The Samaritan woman isn't. She still has her layer of clenched life to be melted; in her case, adultery. So Jesus faces her to it. But don't let that get us off the hook. How hard is it for God to get through to us? If we believe the Living Word has not merely to do with a woman of ancient Samaria, but with our lives, and we notice that Jesus doesn't give her one bit of marriage counseling, then perhaps he wants to help not only her, but through her, all of us? For though adultery means marital infidelity, it's also a metaphor for the way we give ourselves to what is not God, not good, not right, not true. The King James translation of Exodus 34:15 is that people go "a-whoring" after false gods, making what is not good, good and true. Don't we? The metaphor fits, God help us.

And mercifully, God does. Even when we try evasion. Listen to hers: "our people did this, your people did that..." But Christ won't be side-tracked. At this moment, wherever your mind is, Christ points you to the truth, in the noon brightness: "The hour is now: God's way!" In all the activities of your life, God's way: in your attitudes, your job, bedroom, polling booth, tax return — in your heart and spirit — in truth. God's way! Beginning now. It's high noon.

With awareness dawning in her, the woman answers, "I've heard that when Christ comes, he will show us all things." He replies, "I who speak to you am he." And she knows him, now! It sweeps through her, hurting and cleansing and lifting. She turns, forgetting her water pot, hurrying to her people: "Please listen! I learned the truth about myself!" *Kairos*.

Hear what she's saying. It's not: "Now I know the correct religion," but "I learned the truth about me!" *Kairo*s is when you are at last facing yourself in God's illuminating Word. Mind revealed, your inmost spirit open to your own blush and God's forgiveness, you know Christ. You leave your "water pot," the trivial material things that fill the average day, and go out into life with him.

The Samaritan woman would be the last person they'd expect to see filled with God. But she was, they see it, hear it — and there's only one thing they can do. Come out quickly to find who made the difference in her.

So here at Jacob's well, to one after another of the Samaritans, with whom Jews had no dealings, Jesus the Jew, Jesus the Christ, offers the living water, and they drink. So Life came to Sychar; and Sychar comes to life!

At these deep waters cf God's Word, thus may Life come to us, and thus may we come to life. Thus may all God's family become our family and thus may we be empowered to serve them.

Chapter 4: To serve by the Christing of our eyes

Mark 9:2-7:

> ...Jesus took with him Peter and James and John, and led them up a high mountain apart by themselves; and he was transfigured before them, and his garments became glistening, intensely white, as no fuller on earth could bleach them. And there appeared to them Elijah with Moses; and they were talking to Jesus. And Peter said, "Master, it is well that we are here; let us make three tabernacles, one for you and one for Moses and one for Elijah." For he did not know what to say, for they were exceedingly afraid. And a cloud overshadowed them, and a voice came out of the cloud, "This is my beloved Son; listen to him."

It's not always easy to translate the Church's long words into lifting life. How do "sanctification," "ecumenicity" or "eschatology" bring us radiance? They're meant to.

Today, as I write, is August 6th, the Feast of the Transfiguration. This morning I worked for Volunteers of America. Has one any meaning for the other? Can the Transfiguration somehow invigorate us as servants?

Generally, the Christian circles I move in seem to receive Mark 9:2-7 as intriguing, mystic, revered, but — rather irrelevant. Nor does the rest of the account edify much, because life seems to go on just as before. When the disciples come down from their mountaintop experience, a boy convulsed with seizures needs their help. But they can't do a thing for him. Jesus heals the boy. The disciples begin arguing which of them is greatest. So what did they learn? Existentially, the Transfiguration rarely figures much in people's business, pleasure or domestic plans. Would you agree?

But the church promises this experience on the mountain is an empowering way of seeing life, that makes all the difference. We should be open to it then.

Certainly each of us sees life differently, optimists as half full, pessimists as half empty. Some through rose-colored spectacles, some through dark.

John Wesley looked at life through *four* glasses, which he chose very deliberately. He called them a mobile: of Scripture, Reason, Tradition, and Experience. Whenever he struggled with a decision, or what God's will was, he would look at it (1) through the Word of God: what does Scripture seem to say about it? But he'd also ask (2) does this make sense to my brain, to my God-given reason? (3) Is it what the church has believed, my forebears in the faith, people in my tradition whom I respect? (4) Does this accord with my previous personal experience of God in my life? If his decision seemed contradicted by any of the four "tests," he would study further.

I find that helpful. But I'd add a fifth glass through which to look at any decision or attitude, any word or action: does this, which seems to be of God, also accord with Jesus' ministry and commission to us, "Be compassionate, as God is compassionate?" (Luke 6: 36).

Which brings us back to the transfigurating Jesus of Nazareth. Let me offer two incidents from my life that help me understand this event. One is personal, the other scriptural. Both are true.

In 1948 the Allies decided to hold a commemoration of World War II near the former D-Day headquarters of General Eisenhower, at Southsea on the British coast. It was put in charge of the British. They're rather good at parties, and it was their coast.

At the climax, a hero would kindle a "Flame of Freedom" which would be sailed to the D-Day beaches in Normandy.

The hero chosen was Field Marshall Montgomery. The ship chosen was ours: not heroic, but "tiddly," smart, jaunty, trim. I was Executive Officer, our Captain Keith Charles. To his historic task Keith brought three qualities: Royal Navy nonchalance; high school French — useful when we got to France — and a custom tailored Moss Bros. uniform. The Navy gave us soap, paint, brass-polish, and a fortnight to prepare.

At the precise appointed time we arrived at Southsea Pier to behold amazing goings-on: bands blazed, flags waved, ten thousand schoolchildren cheered, ships tooted, Spitfires swooped. We tied to the end of the pier, and came to attention. A dais had been raised on which a clutch of generals was taking turns making speeches. Drums, banners, trumpets, troops, and, on a rickety tower, newsreel cameras recording it: all was superb!

Suddenly, the cacophony quelled. Monty was at the mike, clearing his throat. As if at a bugle call, three giant sergeants of British Paratroops marched to a spot below him, and saluted spectacularly, the middle sergeant bearing an unlit Olympic-type magnesium torch. Sergeants of British Paratroops tend to be formidable: 270 pounds or so, seven feet in their socks. These were huge.

Over the loudspeakers the Field Marshall's voice now boomed words of power: of the memory and the meaning of the brave men who early one morning crossed this sea, and dared, and died. And what privilege was his that on behalf of those who now so honored them, he should kindle the "Flame of Freedom." Glowering down at the sergeants, and beyond them at us, he charged all with its trust. And put a match to the torch. To my surprise — and I'm sure to theirs — a fiery explosion enveloped the generals.

The Paratroopers hadn't moved an eyelash. They saluted, turned, and marched enormously down the pier, torch held aloft by the middle sergeant. Newsreel cameras swung, our stomachs tightened. Then we saw what was happening to that solid oak pier: 700 pounds of sergeant, tromping in unison, were pulsating it up and down: most impressive. Especially to me. I'd extended to the pier a modest gangplank, over which this massive torch-bearer would crunch. I quickly prayed we wouldn't dunk a Flame of Freedom only seconds old. But the plank held, bouncing the sergeant like a heaving hippo (even in mid-air, marching impeccably!) landing him in front of Keith.

At his elegant best, Keith awaited presentation of the Flame. Which the sergeant did, with proper paratroops precision, his arm ramrodding forward, "Zattt!" But someone should have mentioned, at least to Keith, that when one makes paratroop gestures with a magnesium torch, Niagaras of burning bits spray in the direction the gesture is aimed. Our Captain who immediately caught fire in a dozen places — hat, doeskin shoulders, knee, even one shoe was burning.

Did I mention, we were a gasoline-driven ship? Under his feet were 2,000 gallons of high octane. What was so cute was that behind him hung a fierce red notice, "No Smoking Abaft the Funnel!" Keith was smoking well abaft the funnel. A hose quickly put his fires out and he was bundled below, wet but smoldering. A sailor carried the Flame aloft to the bridge, and the cheering started. To the farewells of bands, ships, troops, and planes, we sailed for France.

With Keith below, I now took command. England was soon far astern and I made a first command decision: put the Flame in a hurricane lamp, to curb its incendiary menace. The lamp required a simple two-hourly routine: I'd carry it into the wheel house, devoutly transfer the Flame of Freedom to a fresh wick and container of kerosene, insert them in the lamp, then bear it in an attitude of piety back to the mast. The sea miles passed. And it started getting rough.

At two a.m., with the sea now fighting mad, it was time for my chore. In the wheel-house, I took out the Flame on the little table beside the helmsman, touched it to the new wick, when — BANG! The bow hit a huge wave, the wheel threw the helmsman, the helmsman threw me, and I threw the Flame.

I was a pipe smoker in those days, so whistling a bar of "God Save the King," I relit the Flame of Freedom. Then I noticed the helmsman watching with some interest. My eyes blazed a signal: "Seal your lips, sailor!" And his replied, "Mum's the word, Sir, mum's the word."

Early in the morning the Normandy coast hove in sight. England had done well, but France did better! Rows of ambassadors in sashed uniforms, children and parents by the tens of thousands, armies, brass, princes, Legionnaire bands from all France, filling the heavens. *Magnifique*!

We marched ashore, forming three sides of a little square, surrounded by multitudes. I delivered our Flame, now blazing on a fresh magnesium torch, to the Mayor. He was closing the final speech with "...I now, a humble man, receive, on behalf of Europe, into these very fingers, The Eternal Flame..." I stared across the little square at the other half of the ship's company, and who should stand opposite me but the helmsman of the night before, his face purpling.

"How proud to receive this very Flame, which just yesterday was kindled by the warrior-hero of Europe, Field Marshall Montgomery!" The bulging eyes of the helmsman cried silently, "Not this one, monsieur: this one was lit this morning by Jimmy-the-One." Mine again burned their desperate command, "Never a word, sailor!" And his, running water, replied, "I'll try, sir; but it's 'ard; it's bloomin' 'ard." So far as I know, he's never breathed a word of it, stout fellow.

For years, my thoughts struggled. What had I done? I'd made light and little what was meant to be a tribute to men who gave their lives. When the Flame of Freedom came into my care, this fine and honorable thing became empty and laughable. Anyhow, that's how I saw it. I see it differently now.

I was helped by a healing of Jesus of Nazareth. It's recorded in John 9; a lengthy account, but you should read it. I think it helped me realize, deep down, after all this time, that there's another way of seeing what happened back in the English Channel. What they did at Normandy was so fine, in and of itself, it doesn't hinge on my puny failure: there's freedom in our world because of what they did there. And I've kept their flame alive in my heart, all these years, and will always try to do so — especially, as I can, for people who have no freedom. Here's what happened in John 9 that helped me.

A sightless man crouched in the gutter, felt in the dirt for scraps of garbage, breathed the dust of the trampling crowd, and needed help. Jesus came by and touched his eyes with clay. Actually, the account says, he "anointed" his eyes with clay. "Anointed" has the same root as "Christ," which means, of course, "the anointed one." He "Christed" the man's eyes. How would it be to have *our* eyes "Christed!"

It happened for this man when he accepted the clay of Christ's Word on his sight: "Go, wash in the pool of Siloam." That was a fair distance from his begging spot at Temple Gate, and groping his way there he'd no doubt feel grotesque, daubed with mud that caked in the hot sun. But "he went...and washed." I guess, if a person needs badly enough to change his life, he'll do it the Lord's way, even if he looks ridiculous.

"And he went, and washed, and came back seeing." Hurrying now, eyes wide with excitement! If you had asked him earlier what he longed for most urgently, it wouldn't have been money or possessions, but his sight: now, granted him! "He came back seeing." Light broke all round!

And "the neighbors and those who had seen him before, exclaimed, "Isn't this the man who was born blind? Can't be!" "Of course!" he shouted, "A man called Jesus did it!"

But "they brought to the Pharisees the man who had been born blind." They asked him if he realized Jesus must be a sinner in that he works on the Sabbath? "All I know is, he gave me my sight. He's a prophet of God!" Their hearts chilled. Might others also come to see this subversive Galilean as God's prophet? So they did what such people always do when there is no moral power in their case. They used force. "They cast him out."

And there in the lonely place, the man with Christed eyes wandered. No one offered a hand, or gave water for his dry lips. But Jesus found him. And asked, "Do you believe in the Son of Man?" What kind of question is that? You'd think Jesus might have offered help? But that could wait: this couldn't! "Do you believe in the Son of Man?" Answer this right, and everything makes sense! And he did. He who used to be in the dirt and useless now stood with Christed eyes beside his Lord, ready for the world! Changed, inside. Changed, in insight — changed in the way he saw things. First, he'd seen Jesus merely as a great human being: "A man called Jesus did it!" Then, his eyes opening, he could see "a prophet of God!" But as he came to total clarity, full potential, he knew Jesus as Christ. And his life began again.

That's how, for me, not only the Flame of Freedom, but far more important, the Transfiguration really gets home. It's the same kind of sight-healing. Mark tells us that just before the Transfiguration, Jesus had asked his disciples, "Who do men say that I am?" They answer, some say you are, John the Baptist; others, one of the prophets. But "who do *you* say that I am?" "You are the Christ of God!" It's the same healing sequence, the same transformation as the blind man experienced in John 9! So Jesus can now tell them how he must suffer, and be killed, and be raised from the dead; that whoever will come with him, must follow in the path of servant and sufferer. His words sink deep into them, so that when they look again at Jesus, now they see him transfigured, the appearance of his countenance altered, his raiment dazzling. And their lives begin! Their serving like Christ begins!

Can we modern materialists know what really happened on the Mount of Transfiguration? Something happened. It wasn't only a matter of their eyes. In Exodus 34, as Moses climbed the mountain to receive the Commandments, the nearness of God made his skin glow, such that Aaron and the people held back in awe at sight of him. God's presence shone from his face.

Does anything in our experience let us see things like that? Once, Renee and I went to see Richard Burton in *Camelot*. He came from Wales, just down the river Afan from me. So he invited us to meet backstage. But he wasn't Richard Burton yet. He was still King Arthur, the kingship in his bearing and eyes luminous with majesty. It took him minutes to come down to being Dickie Burton from the valleys, dragging on a cigarette, asking home news. (So it wasn't King Arthur who kissed Renee farewell on the cheek, just Dickie Burton. But she enjoyed it anyway.) The question is, though, if mere Burton could glow as he did, could not Christ, just once, convey the aura of that eternal world of light that was in him? I'm sure of it.

Afterwards, down into the valley go the disciples. They fail faithlessly at the healing work so needed of them. They fail bitterly as loving comrades. But having seen Jesus as the Christ, their own transformation has begun.

That's what Transfiguration means: as Jesus becomes transfigured in your eyes, you become transformed in his. As you see how Jesus is your Christ, he sees how you can be his Christian. Christ looks into our eyes, sees his light and love reflected there, and knows what they can make us. The mountaintop experience is not some ancient mysticism, but each day's empowerment. We can hear his "Yes!" to our lifting lives! His Word anoints our eyes, and he sees us as his fellow servants.

And makes us so.

Chapter 5: Our ears open and we speak plain

Mark 7:31-37:

> Then (Jesus) returned from the region of Tyre, and went through Sidon to the sea of Galilee, through the region of the Decapolis. And they brought to him a man who was deaf and had an impediment in his speech; and they besought him to lay his hand upon him. And taking him aside from the multitude privately, he put his fingers into his ears, and he spat and touched his tongue; and looking up to heaven, he sighed, and said to him, "Be opened." And his ears were opened, his tongue was released, and he spoke plainly.

What has this Scripture to do with us? There was a man of Decapolis, deaf and with a speech impediment. You'd have to stretch the point a long way, wouldn't you, to fit our situation?

But as I opened Ballington Booth's New Testament to Mark 7, I was surprised to find that he had written all over it. He rarely wrote on his Bible. Yet this text he'd not only underlined, but summarized in ink in the margin, and even tried to highlight by writing over the text in ink! Obviously this passage meant a great deal to him. So perhaps we should stretch the point, and see if it fits even a little.

My first Volunteers of America board meeting, I was asked to give the Invocation. Business began, and the range and quality of services offered was immediately impressive. They had given us newcomers orientation materials, which as we listened and learned, I tried to leaf through. Near the bottom of the pile was the national Mission Statement. It says we are:

> "...a movement organized to reach and uplift all people and bring them to the knowledge and active service of God. Volunteers of America, illustrating the presence of God through all that we do, serves people and communities in need and creates opportunities for people to experience the joy of serving others."

This was interesting because we had already looked at our local Mission Statement. Crisp and clear, it affirmed that we "promote self-sufficiency by providing social services and by strengthening the community." No reference to God. Come to think of it, there had been no reference to God since the Invocation. Well, it seemed brash to raise it, so I didn't.

Back home, my trusty Encarta Encyclopedia described Volunteers of America as a "nonsectarian philanthropic organization." Didn't anyone tell the editors it's a church with several hundred ministers? So at the next meeting I did mention it. And there seemed almost relief that someone had, because in the many discussions that have followed, we've agreed, we're missing something important.

The fact is, from the moment of its founding in 1896, Volunteers of America was first and foremost a church. I'll return to that, but let me note another historical fact. This new church's ministry was remarkable both for its swift surging extensions across the entire nation, and also for the public acclaim soon flowing from both poor and mighty. The pages of Wisbey's history, for example, imply astonishment at "the very speed at which the movement grew" (p. 28): it "mushroomed from an idea to a nationwide organization almost overnight" (p. 46). In the first two years emergency work became strikingly effective in all parts of the country.

Longer-term service programs were begun in Ithaca, Syracuse, Youngstown, and Los Angeles. In 1899, Newark, New Jersey saw the first Volunteers of America home for unmarried mothers; in Buffalo a "Faith Home" to rescue outcast girls in the city's slums; in Bridgeport, Connecticut, a salvage and rehabilitation program where:

> "...men applying for food and lodging were obliged to work in the woodyard. Their task, which they could finish in ninety minutes, entitled them to one meal and one night's lodging." Clothing was collected for those who came in rags. Although hampered by lack of funds, 2,981 lodgings and 2,510 meals were provided in the first year" (W. p. 59).

By the turn of the century the movement had, in four short years, become a national social relief agency, fully organized and effective as a church from coast to coast. Gratitude for its ministry was swift and widespread. This letter from a convict is typical:

> *I want to thank you and the Volunteers of America for the wonderful gifts you have sent to my family for Christmas...With your help my kids had a better Christmas...please pray for me and my family (W. p.76).*

The famous and wealthy also embraced the ministry. As Wisbey notes (p. 42), Ballington Booth's address book, beginning under the A's with Vincent Astor, included Bernard Baruch, Walter Damrosch, Bishop Manning, Rabbi Stephen Wise, John D. Rockefeller, Alfred Vanderbilt, and John Wanamaker. He could count on the support of many great leaders in business, government, and religion. One of the nation's most prominent clergyman, Rev. Josiah Strong, pioneer of the Social Gospel, applauded the Volunteers because "I believe in the principles on which the movement is based." President Theodore Roosevelt and William Jennings Bryant were its friends, and endorsed its work.

Wisbey records Ballington's good relationship with President Woodrow Wilson (p. 93f), and with Andrew Mellon, who affirmed the Volunteer ministry as "a potent force in building up a Christian civilization in America" (p. 102); with President Warren Harding, who wrote, "There are few parallels in history where husband and wife have jointly and severally made such a notable contribution to human uplift" (p. 101). Rabbi Wise, a friend of Volunteers of America from its start, after the death of Maud Booth in 1948 wrote to her son,

> *...Your Mother was a lovely being, as lovely in herself as in her work, the beauty of her spirit shining through her eyes...I need hardly tell you how great and noble a spirit she was, how much she did for others... (W. p. 45).*

The rapid spread and effectiveness of the serving ministry, and its wide public recognition, the founders attributed to God's Spirit at work in them. They tried to live out the ministry of Jesus, work and

Word; and God's Spirit empowered them. Not only was Christ's work done, but the Word took wing. To reverse a bit of modern street speech, they not only walked the walk, they talked the talk...of Christ!

Is it our concern that we're mainly walking the walk? Truly, we're doing it well. Our forebears would be proud. But the Word is not much on our lips, and we so need it. Our ministry does, and our world does.

Of course, if you had to choose between doing the work of Christ and saying the words, the choice is easy. Jesus (Matt 21:28ff) poses it like this: a man sent his two sons to the fields; one refused, but did it; the other agreed, but didn't do it. We have no doubt which is approved. Even more poignantly Jesus asks, "Why do you call me 'Lord,' and do not do what I tell you?" (Luke 6:46)

But we don't have to choose. Our work needs both the actions of love and the Word which enables them. And there's no doubt that the founders committed themselves to both. Both Maud and Ballington Booth saw themselves first and mainly as preachers of the Gospel. Their deeds poured out as fruit of the Word.

Someone said of Maud Booth, "When she spoke there was a halo round her head," yet "her aim was to get her audience to forget her and listen only to her message" (W. p. 68). By 1900, she'd become "one of the most popular and highest paid women lecturers...and all of the proceeds of her speaking tours went to finance her prison work" (W. p. 67). And the Word within her words? To the convicts, for example, she knew,

> "...What they needed from my lips was...something that would carry their thoughts away beyond the gray walls and some message from Christ's dear heart of love that would part the dark clouds and show a pure ray of light and comfort from Hope's true star" (W. p. 63).

And the Word apparently had wings, because "...men would brave the jeers and laughter of their fellow prisoners to stand up and signify publicly their desire to lead a new life with God's help and through His salvation" (W. p. 63).

Her husband was recognized as "one of the outstanding preachers of the day by a generation that had listened to Henry Ward Beecher, T. DeWitt Talmage, Dwight Moody, and Phillips Brooks" (W. p. 77).

I'm looking again at his New Testament. In it, among his handwritten notes of sermons, are his records of the places he preached the Gospel. I count 230 entries, including every major city in the United States, and small towns I never heard of. His lifelong testimony is reflected in his final address to the Grand Field Council, at age 79:

> *My outstanding thought as I face you...is one that has ever been uppermost with me, the desire to bring men and women to the knowledge of our blessed Lord. I want...to be a soul-winner; I want the years left me to witness men and women at the spot I love to see them — at the feet of Jesus Christ. My whole heart is close to Him as I think, talk, and read about Him*" (W. p. 118).

And as we've seen, at least two of the major consequences of their speaking the Word were an incredible increase, across the land, in programs of service, and a matching national outpouring of gratitude.

It seems full time that we successors turn again to their source. We need the Word for our own sake, and for the work's sake. We need to hear the Word for the enabling of our ministry; and we need to speak the Word to lift people's lives.

So let's allow into our lives this Decapolis man, who can't hear or speak properly, brought to Christ for healing. Perhaps he doesn't speak properly because he doesn't hear properly. If he hasn't heard the words spoken, is it that he doesn't know how to reproduce them? And if he tries, maybe the words come out as harsh, unpleasant grunts or silly jibber-jabber. Jesus draws him apart from the crowd where they can be privately together, and lays his hands on his ears. It's a kind of sign language, helping the man realize he knows what's wrong. Put yourself in the Decapolis man's place; you're now aware Christ is present, knows your problem, and wants to help.

After all, how much distress is due to our not hearing a nearby heart breaking, or someone biting a lip in pain, or the sound of a sob; or, a little farther off, the shivering of a person who has no home or coat? There's much deafness to the crucial sounds God wants us to hear, to both the Word and the hurts. There are many Decapolis people.

And Jesus touches the man's tongue. Sign language again: "He knows I don't speak properly." Then Jesus looks up to heaven, and the sign language is utterly clear: What is about to happen is of God. He does one more thing. He sighs deeply, like a prayer. And so he enters our situation. We know we're not alone in this any more. He has lifted it upon himself.

So will you now hear the Word of blessing, "be opened?" God's grace brings healing. Believe it! For in precisely the same way as the life-filled Word touches the man, it touches us. That we may hear as he means us to, as Christpeople! "Be opened," Jesus says. If you'll listen in your heart, hearing begins. Better than ever, we'll hear a tear running down a face, here...silent grief, over there...pain, hunger, wrong. We'll be open to hearing the Word of God that lifts our lives, and empowers us to lift life.

And touching our tongues, the Word says "be opened." And we can *speak* now what God wants us to say, the true, great words that echo his gracious Word of peace and compassion, joy and meaning. Respond to him, and our voices will free and we can speak mercy, hope, and justice. We can be the gentle ones who bring love's service to our communities.

It doesn't always happen all at once, this miracle of the Word. Years ago, Renee and I taught Sunday School at a little Methodist Church in Cornwall. We remembered gratefully John Wesley's advice to young ministers: "Preach faith until you have it!" That's not as suspect as it sounds. If as faithfully as you can, you speak the Word, it will take wing in you, also. Having each Sunday to tell of Christ to a gang of rambunctious youngsters, meant we had to get it right, as appealingly as we knew how, praying some of it got through to them. And some of it got through to us!

We never heard God's Word in any "supernatural" fashion. Sometimes, in prayer, or in struggling with the Scripture, or in a hymn or sermon, there would come a quiet, holy idea, deep down, making itself heard. And if we listened, and if we responded, it translated itself into action in us, and came out as a new behavior, an increase in love, and a holier life.

Later, when I was ordained, it was now my terrifying and wonderful task to try to interpret the Word faithfully to my congregation on Sunday mornings. May I take a moment to tell you how, if God pleases, it happens?

On *Monday*, I'll read the chosen scripture, and try to understand. I try not to search the commentaries to find what others think, but myself, in the depths in me, committing it to the Holy Spirit. On *Tuesday*, I read it several times more; do the scholarly work. Who wrote it, when, to whom, for what purpose, in what context? Then I put it all back for the nurturing of the Spirit, deep within. By *Wednesday*, I'm praying for insight. But it's a struggle, now. Will God's Spirit show me what it is, does, how it helps? Am I getting in its way? Are old ideas or old experiences impeding what is the healing truth, and the words to express it?

Thursday, surely, light begins to come. I find human language for God's Word; or life is tense! By *Friday*, the response must form? Test, reexamine: this is God's Word we're speaking of! Is His Spirit in this? Intensify, all *Saturday*: please God, don't make me throw it all away, now: nevertheless, not my will, but thine, be done.

But if what is heard on *Sunday* is from "the Word made flesh who dwells among us, full of grace and truth," then we're getting the Word live: getting it straight! The same mighty Word of God through which all things were made, from earliest human understanding, now speaks in our spirits! And, if we will, gets through: as an ideal, or as a deep feeling, or an imperative to act, or the empowerment to serve.

To my friends in the Volunteers of America I say, make opportunities to hear and speak the Word. Gather a group of colleagues sometimes for a word of prayer or a reading of Scripture, discussion, fellowship, sharing what's in your hearts. If we as a church, in the posture of the

Decapolis man, will ask our Lord for ability to hear the Word, and speak it, it will be done. For surely, in its own good time, the Word does come through. God's grace and our response come together. His loving gift of Spirit and our enabled life of service combine.

That's the Gospel.

Chapter 6: Deeper than our hearts

Matthew 25:31-46.

> *"When the Son of man comes in his glory, and all the angels with him, then he will sit on his glorious throne. Before him will be gathered all the nations, and he will separate them one from another as a shepherd separates the sheep from the goats, and he will place the sheep at his right hand, but the goats at the left. Then the King will say to those at his right hand, 'Come, O blessed of my Father, inherit the kingdom prepared for you from the foundation of the world; for I was hungry and you gave me food, I was thirsty and you gave me drink, I was a stranger and you welcomed me, I was naked and you clothed me, I was sick and you visited me, I was in prison and you came to me.' Then the righteous will answer him, 'Lord, when did we see thee hungry and feed thee, or thirsty and give thee drink? And when did we see thee a stranger and welcome thee, or naked and clothe thee? And when did we see thee sick or in prison and visit thee?' And the King will answer them, 'Truly, I say to you, as you did it to one of the least of these my brethren, you did it to me.' Then he will say to those at his left hand, 'Depart from me, you cursed, into the eternal fire prepared for the devil and his angels; for I was hungry and you gave me no food, I was thirsty and you gave me no drink, I was a stranger and you did not welcome me, naked and you did not clothe me, sick and in prison and you did not visit me.' Then they also will answer, 'Lord, when did we see thee hungry or thirsty or a stranger or naked or sick or in prison, and did not minister to thee?' Then he will answer them, 'Truly, I say to you, as you did it not to one of the least of these, you did it not to me.' And they will go away into eternal punishment, but the righteous into eternal life."*

This parable of the last judgment is Jesus' summation of his teaching. The heart of it is that we are to care for "the least." For Matthew, it's the final briefing. Soon, Jesus will be gone. So much will depend on those who understand his teaching, living it. It will mean much to those "least" whose lives are anguished, but much, too, to those who care for them, and find blessing and eternal life.

This weighs heavy on me. Let me say why. One night, in a thick fog, the Royal Navy minesweeper of which I was navigator got an S.O.S. from a wrecked tanker. My job was to locate her, so her injured sailors could be brought aboard and rushed to hospital. Navigating through night fog was tense for a 20-year-old. After harassed hours, I found the sinking ship.

Swiftly, they brought the wounded below. One sailor was so badly injured, they dared not tilt him down a ladder. On the upper deck the only shelter available was my six-feet-by-four chartroom, which really had space only for me and my equipment. So they put his stretcher there, between my feet. I had just room to straddle him, one foot on either side. He was my age, or maybe younger, 19.

We started the difficult voyage home: difficult especially for me, finding a way back through a dark pillow of fog, with the added pressure of smashed-up sailors urgently needing help. And I was irritated at this enlisted man under my feet, his makeshift bandages seeping blood, making the deck slippery.

He seemed to have massive internal stomach damage. The side of his head was smashed. A leg seemed broken. He could hardly breathe. But he could still speak, and kept trying. Every few minutes, I'd have to put down my navigational instruments and wipe clots of blood from his mouth with my handkerchief. He was lucky I had time for that. My hands and the chart were soon bloody.

He struggled to talk. He tried to tell me about himself, about his home, his dad and two small sisters, his church. He'd been in the youth choir. I was too busy to answer. But he went on whispering to me. I wished he would shut up. In the fog it was hard to find buoy after buoy. And there was all that blood.

Perhaps it may have dawned on me, deep down, what he was trying to tell me: that he was afraid he was going to die and wanted someone to be friendly to him, so he wouldn't end like a crushed insect. But if I did suspect it, I never let the thought up into my mind. I still wanted him out of my chartroom, rationalizing I couldn't do my job — which meant we wouldn't get him or the others ashore in time — with him interrupting me, bleeding and whispering.

We were two miles from shore when he died. He asked me for a cigarette. But I was a pipe smoker. A frightened look came on that bruised face, and his life left him. I navigated the last two miles with my eyes full. The way I treated that young sailor still haunts me. For years, I've been ashamed. He was my brother, and I denied him. He was one of "the least" God put in my life, and I did not care for him.

I tell myself I was young, then. I have cared for many since. Surely one long-ago avoidance doesn't decide it? Yet, sometimes, that wounded sailor's face still looks frightened up at me. Is he pointing in my life to those "least" who despair in my town, victims of racism, poverty, and ignorance? Or those alone in a nursing home, or the homeless? Or those starving in a distant African country or the million underaged in out-of-sight sweatshops? Who cares? I know I should.

I need grace.

Here is my hope. Jesus lived to the full his own teaching always unfailingly caring for the least. But always, there was compassion and always, there was grace. Grace is God's love freely given, entirely unmerited. This is my hope.

Imagine this scene. Into one of the dark alleys of Jerusalem some men have taken a young woman. Suddenly there are shouts, bright sunlight, and she's dragged through the crowds, struggling and dazed, clothes awry. Flung painfully down in the sunlit sand, she peers frightened through her matted hair. There's a man sitting on the steps of the Temple. They have brought her to the Temple before this man who is looking at her with a troubled expression.

"Teacher, this woman was caught in the act of adultery. In the law, Moses commanded us to stone such. What do you say about her?" She is the trap they have set for him. If in his pity for her, he urges she be spared, he'll be denying holy law; uphold it, and he loses the regard of the people who love him for his mercy. She looks up at him. There's no disgust in his face, though; only concern. Then he turns to them, his eyes shaming them: "He that is without sin among you, throw the first stone." One by one they slink away.

She cries into the dirt. He lifts her, and asks quietly, "Where are your accusers? Has no one condemned you?" She tries to speak: "No one, Lord." "Nor do I condemn you; go, and sin no more." Touching her face to wipe the sand away, he lets her go. And her life begins (John 8:2 - 11).

That's the grace I need.

The insane came to him, diseased people, the twisted. And though none could say how, each found bright eyes, clean flesh, straight limbs. He lifted the most undeserving most tenderly: "Come to me, you heavy laden." Shifty businessmen, a glib civil servant, drunks abandoned all that and followed him. That's the kind of grace I need.

He was all love.

Peter learned that. It's so fundamental for Peter, he didn't just write, "have fervent love," but "above all things, have fervent love" (1 Pet 4: 8). John learned it, too; and put it the most plainly: "God is love!" (1 John 4: 8). They got it straight from their Lord: "Be compassionate, as God is compassionate" (Luke 6:36).

Paul was sure of it. Read 1 Corinthians 13! What is the greatest thing in life — of our traditions, in our relationships, in spiritual gifts? What is God really like? Of course Paul knew how vital faith is: that God is gracious and loving, and was in Christ; that Christ lives, and is in us. Of course he knew how vital hope is: for health, for dear ones, that God has a good purpose for us here, and a greater one beyond...so much to hope for. Every life gift is precious: education, wisdom, good deeds, piety. But from Christ he knew that love is greater than all.

It's in light of this love that I can bear to hear Jesus' last teaching. To be sure, because we hear his final question of our faith clearly framed in terms of justice, "What did you do for the least?" we take it to heart as crucial. And to make certain we know the truth of it, he took a towel and washed their feet: "Now you know. You call me Teacher and Lord; and I am. And I've washed your feet. You do the same." Faith is not only loving and trusting God. With your own hands, faith is taking a towel.

After this, Jesus turned his face to Jerusalem. Soon, soldiers are hammering nails through his hands. He doesn't wrench away, but opens them in pardon. If salvation is all grace, and ethics all gratitude, surely we've gratitude enough now to live as he asked us to.

It's more enabling even than that. Because it's not our love, but God's, that's the key; not what we can't do, but what God can and does! He "so loved the world, he gave his son…"(John 3:16) God knows we can't love the way we need to, either for our own blessing or for helping the least. So God says, "Behold Jesus. This is the way I love." And it's like when we were children in science class. You'd take a bit of dead steel, stroke it with a magnet and before long the steel too became magnetic. You could shape iron filings any way you wanted. Well, God's love in Jesus infuses us if we will, so we now shape into what God wants us to be.

This is how God does it. He opens to us the Scriptures about Jesus, saying: "Experience my love, here, time and again; until one day, loving forms in your brain and your being as the main thing in you. And then, you're doing it!" We experience it as Jesus touches the leper or eats with outcasts or blesses children. The living Word of compassion releases from its restrictions our basic reality, way below all that's wrong, twisted, misunderstood: our capacity to love. As we open ourselves, God's love inspires this greatest thing in life: "We love because he first loved us" (1 John 4:10). It is not an order, "*you shall love*," but a promise, "you *shall* love!" Not a command to care, but a full-fillment!

I well remember how God's Word helped Renee and me. She and I, thank God, are life partners. We just missed being childhood sweethearts. She was 15, I was 16 when we met. In a sense we even missed being teenage ones, in that war time Britain desperately promoted children to adulthood. We recently had the joy of our Fiftieth Anniversary, and I toasted her with, "this was our best year ever!" She agreed, but added, "and you've always said that." Strictly speaking, that's not true; there was a time when life was not so good, when she, a back-slid Baptist and I, a back-slid Episcopalian, blundered about some. But one evening, out of the blue, she asked me to go to a worship service with her, and we went. It happened to be a Methodist church. During worship, the minister read Luke 15, about the Prodigal Son, and witnessed to it. And it came home to us both, how much we mean to God. In Jesus' enabling words we experienced that evening the father's love. Heart aching for the boy in the far country, he watches each day the long road to the hills. The boy's done wrong, but he's his child. He loves him and that's all that matters. When at last he sees him in the distance, coming home, how he runs to meet him, arms round him, won't listen to his apology, kissing him, all the hurt of longing over. Jesus draws us into a love like that.

Like what? Jesus taught and lived out the scripture. "Be compassionate, as God is compassionate." Luke's Hebrew word for "compassion" is the plural, *rachamim*; the singular, *racham*, means "womb." That's the love! So deep, it's as from the womb of God, who created each of us, nourishes us, cares for us: this *is* how a mother loves the children of her womb. This is how a man loves his brother, who came from the same womb. This *is* how God has always loved us!

To live out that love is what God has always asked of us through his Word. Through Ezekiel, "strengthen the weak... seek the lost" (Ez. 34:3); in the Psalms, "secure justice for the...afflicted; rescue...the needy" (Ps. 82:3, ff.); in the prophets Hosea, Jeremiah, Micah. Until at last Jesus can hear those who would be his ask him, "Lord, when was it we saw you hungry and fed you, a stranger and took you home, naked and clothed you?" And he can answer, "When you did it for the least." That's what we're to do, and can do now in our grimy world. Love works.

I recall a touching old account of a little girl, back in the hills, whose mother died when she was eight. Her father was an alcoholic who couldn't hold a job. There were five other children still younger than she, whom she tried to care for. Up before light, work till after dark, she struggled on. Until she was used up. This tiny old lady at 11 got tuberculosis and began to die.

A neighbor woman climbed the hill to sit with her and share her troubles. The girl's wizened little face pained. She said, "I don't think I'm afraid; but I am ashamed." "How could you be?" the older one asked.

"Well, when mother passed, she made me promise to take the children every week to worship. But I haven't... It's been so hard. When I meet our Father, what can I tell him?" The woman, holding back her tears, took the little callused hands in hers, and said: "I shouldn't tell him anything, dear...just show him your hands."

How surprised she will be, and how blessed.

Perhaps the girl comes to mind now because I've just returned from the national meeting of the Volunteers of America. It was a profound theological experience. As a churchman of ripe years, I've attended many church conferences but never one like this. From all over the U.S. gathered men and women I've come to recognize as superb professionals, expert at helping people, dedicated to doing so, who nevertheless, it seemed, were searching for their souls. Like the girl, they've not attended much to churchy things but now are asking, "what shall I tell him?" One wants to answer, "Just show him your hands." But an even greater answer was there.

It began with a sermon by Father Fred Kammer. He is a Jesuit lawyer-priest, national president of Associated Catholic Charities, and advocate for the poor and powerless. He is also the author of a book called *Doing Faithjustice*. His sermon explicated it and was a transforming experience. Here is essential Gospel truth, usually avoided, whose avoidance eviscerates Christ's minister, and ours.

Faithjustice is "a passionate virtue which disposes citizens to become involved in the greater and lesser societies around themselves in order to create communities where human dignity is protected and enhanced, the gifts of creation are shared for the greatest good of all, and the poor are cared for with respect and a special love." Kammer led us from God's elicitation of faithjustice in people even before the Bible, through Israel's clear response to it, and finally through Jesus' work and teaching and to his enabling it in us. It was an elevating revelation. We knew ourselves rooted in the vital tradition and felt our own commitment lift and firm.

His book begins with a December 1978 article from *National Geographic* about an archeological dig in northwestern Syria and clay tablets from the 3000 BC. city-state of Ebla: "Eblaites believed their leaders should be accessible and accountable. A king ascended the throne not strictly through lineage but by election, and was responsible for the welfare of widows, the orphaned, and the poor. If derelict, a king could be ousted." He suggests the Ebla find "may contribute most significantly to our understanding of the Hebrew scriptures," where, of course, there is crucial concern for the widows, the orphaned, and the poor (in Hebrew, the *anawim*).

In those scriptures he discerns three clear understandings of God's call to faithjustice, each a "sharing of some aspect of God's own truth and life, which in turn reveals to us a corresponding aspect of our own truth." First, God's creation is good — all God's creation, including the *anawim* (Gen. 1:31). Second, man and woman are given dominion over, the care of, and the responsibility for, all on earth (Gen. 1:28): including the *anawim*. Third, God chooses to be part of the human community: "I will be your God and you shall be my people" (Lev. 26:12): God identifies with all, including the *anawim*; all are kin to God, so none are to be rejected.

The treatment of the *anawim* throughout the Old Testament is the measure of fidelity to God. Those who do not do justice to them show that they do not know God. They are atheists. And in the Biblical story, they often predominate.

So Kammer leads us to the ministry of Jesus. Straight from his baptism, filled with the Spirit, Jesus returns to his home synagogue at Nazareth, stands, and read Isaiah's announcement: "The spirit of the Lord is upon me…he has sent me to bring glad tidings to the poor, to proclaim liberty to captives…Today this scripture is fulfilled in your hearing." From the start, the treatment of the *anawim* is central to Jesus' ministry, and still the test of fidelity. The Sermon on the Mount proclaims that he will devote his life to them, that he belongs to them. Throughout Jesus' teachings and actions, his care for and self-identity with the *anawim* are clear. Blessed are those "who see him in them and reach out to him in them."

And finally, Kammer brings us to our own time and ministry, what he calls "the Age of the Spirit,"

> *The Spirit of God empowers and enables our fidelity and service, a fierce passion for the* anawim *and for justice because it has its source in and flows from the hearts of Abba God and Jesus. The Spirit creates faithjustice anew in the chaos of our time just as the Spirit of God hovered over the waters of Genesis, generated the new creation born in the assent of the young woman Mary of Nazareth, and boldly recreated the disciples of Jesus in the power of Pentecost. Come Holy Spirit, come.*

Amen! And it struck a bell in the listening Volunteers. A church bell, perhaps? This is their inheritance! And not only from the Word of God, but from our church's story. For as one reads the founding ministries, faithjustice is manifest and manifold. As Volunteers of America looks back on a hundred years of service, and ahead to the third millennium, this inheritance lifts us. May that passionate virtue, deeper than the heart — from our *rachamim*, from the depth of our nature with God — empower us to serve the least, sharing the gifts of creation, and caring for them with respect and a special love.

Chapter 7: To serve by enabling prayer

From Matthew 6:9-13:

> *Our Father who art in heaven,*
> *Hallowed be thy name.*
> *Thy kingdom come,*
> *Thy will be done,*
> *On earth as it is in heaven.*
> *Give us this day our daily bread;*
> *And forgive us our debts,*
> *As we also have forgiven our debtors;*
> *And lead us not into temptation,*
> *But deliver us from evil.*
> *For thine is the kingdom*
> *And the power and the glory,*
> *Forever.*
> *Amen.*

In "the powerhouse of prayer" even poets are awed. Tennyson believed, "more things are wrought by prayer than this world dreams of," Cowper said that "Satan trembles when he sees the weakest saint upon his knees." Prayer moves the hand that moves the universe.

Then why is it that often when we begin the Lord's Prayer, our mind slips into automatic and it's a barren exercise? At its worst, habitual praying can remind us of Peter O'Toole's character in "The Ruling Class," who thinks he's Jesus Christ; when asked when this started, he answers, "I was praying and I realized I was talking to myself." But even at the best of our prayer times, it's easy to be distracted, isn't it?

Yet throughout history, people of faith — including Jesus of Nazareth — promise us that surer than anything else we do, true prayer can bring us to a lifting life. Now, I'm no mystic dreamer. Whether as sea captain or college president, I tended to avoid fantasy. But I believe them. So how can we pray true prayer?

Like you, perhaps, I was about three when mother taught me bedtime praying of "Our Father." And at least in this, I was her obedient son. I prayed in that beloved boyhood home, at haughty Cambridge, on British warships, and later, in American bedrooms and college chapels. Often, it did seem to make a difference to how life went. But often, too, it was fruitless rote, and dismaying.

Then I came upon an old rendition of the Lord's Prayer. Its history is uncertain, and we don't know which early Christians used it. But it's been such a Godsend to me, I share it gladly:

> *Life-giver in the light realms, invoking thy name, thy realms appear,*
> *And thy will is performed on the earth, as it is done in the light realms.*
> *Give us thy food for the coming day,*
> *And forgive our transgressions, even as we forgive our transgressors.*
> *Bring us not to the test, but deliver us from the opposing powers.*
> *For of thee are the realms, and the energies, and the radiances,*
> *Throughout the life cycles, eternally, forever. Amen.*

That's how I start every day. And as the phrases are spoken, often the corresponding words of the beloved "Our Father" seem to undergird them. At night, I pray "Our Father" and the phrases of the morning prayer echo and strengthen. Both seem often true prayer.

First thing in the morning, though, I'm not very spiritual. I need a bit of extra help to pray from that deep "inner closet" where true prayer is done. So I kneel at a little prayer-desk, homemade years ago by a friend. At night, tiredness encourages prayer in the bedroom, but early or late, kneeling, in bedroom or church, walking, standing, wherever, true prayer lifts life.

"True prayer" is at the deepest level in us. Again, think of Psalm 42: 7, "when deep calls to deep:" a cry from our depths to the depth of God links our human spirit profoundly with the Holy Spirit. Of course, most often in human experience, it's not our pleading but the Deep of God speaking in our deep, that makes the healing initiative.

Recall how Jacob heard it in Genesis 28:

> *Jacob...came to a certain place, and stayed there that night, because the sun had set. Taking one of the stones of the place, he put it under his head and lay down in that place to sleep. And he dreamed that there was a ladder set up on the earth, and the top of it reached to heaven; and the angels of God were ascending and descending on it. And behold, the Lord stood above it and said, "I am the Lord, the God of Abraham your father and the God of Isaac; the land on which you lie I will give to you and to your descendants; and your descendants shall be like the dust of the earth."*

Awake from his dream, Jacob responds as to a divine initiative with a vow of faithfulness and the building of a house to God. Then he journeys on until he comes to a well (there's that symbol of depth again), and his new life begins. It was so with Noah and Abraham. God spoke first, and they responded, and found their worlds changed, as did Moses and Isaiah and the Prophets. Surely, that's how God gets his work done, speaking perhaps quietly in a still, small voice within, or through some Word, or through one of his servants who interprets the Word — in all times, in all people, in every person, deep to deep. Some want to hear, and do hear. Then what God has spoken rises from way down in the soul, out into the life of the hearer.

You can observe it all through Scripture. Time and again, someone will realize what God wants done and cry out, "The Word of the Lord came upon me," or "Thus says the Lord," and embark on the voyage of faith and new life. God's Word and human response — that's how God's work gets done!

True prayer, deep to deep, unclenches our soul so we can hear God's affirmation. Listen to Isaiah 41:10 in the Hebrew Bible, and the King James: God says, "Yes, I will help you; yes, I will uphold you!" "Yes!" In Isaiah 46:11 God says, "Yes, I have spoken it!" God is fundamentally one who affirms. Of course, at times God must say "No." So many of our attitudes and acts require and receive a "Never!" But deeper than our distortions and defeats, at the heart of the universe is the affirmation of a loving God. Time and again, God says, "I will!" "I will redeem you." "I will comfort you." "I will lead you…" Ours is a God who says, "I will!" Yes!

Jesus gives his Word on it: "Ask, and it will be given you" (Mt. 7:7 and Luke 11:9). That's a "Yes!" "Whatever you ask in prayer, you will receive!" (Mt. 21:22). That's a "Yes!" "Your Father knows what you need before you ask him!" (Mt. 6:8) That's a "Yes!" in advance! These are the Words of God!

Here's another fact about true prayer: it transforms us. When you pray true prayer, deep to deep, in his Word, and out of his truth, then with the "Yes!" of our loving Lord comes his empowerment to work with him in it. Two children quarreled: the boy had set a bird trap in the garden, and his little sister was horrified at his cruelty. That night, in her prayers, she asked that her brother not kill any birds in his trap, and hopped into bed with a happy smile. Her mother, tucking her in, asked why the smile? "God's going to answer my prayer." "How can you be sure?" "Well, before we came up, I went and smashed that old bird trap." True praying smashes the distinction between our talk and our deeds.

So to our praying of The Lord's Prayer. Imagine people who are in pain or distress. Their praying might well be for healing of their personal anguish. That's obviously proper and important. If you were dreadfully ill, you'd pray to be healed and Scripture teaches so. From the deepest in you, you'd pray, *"Our Father."* And as you pray it, deep to deep, reaching out pleadingly, suddenly again you're experiencing God as your loving Father and your own true being as his son or his daughter! It's like a moment of re-creation, in which you see yourself as you were meant to be, the prayer now not only about your heavenly Father, but showing you yourself as God's dearly loved child.

Certainly, if I'm in anguish when night comes, that's what I pray happens. Or in the morning, praying deep as I can *"Life giver in the light realms"* as the true words make a sudden expansion of my spirit, I experience God afresh as life-giver — and myself as life-receiver. "Yes!"

If we truly pray *"Thy will be done,"* there it is! The truth, true for us! God's will, invincible in our lives! So we don't need to try manipulating God to get our own way. Praying in his Spirit turns upward the chalice of our being to receive the life God is pouring out on us all the time. The prayer isn't trying to convert God to our way. It opens our spirit to God's, which is the best anyone could ever want, or ever have.

"Thy will is performed," I pray each morning. It is not a resigned sigh, but a shout of joy! What our loving Father wants for us, his dear children, will be. "Yes!" Now we're empowered to work with God, for healing, wholeness, exhilaration! God answers prayer, always; the question is do you accept the "Yes!" — the power and the love always streaming to us from our Father?

Or as our Volunteer morning begins, and many people depend on our work of service being effectively done, we pray *"Our Father, who art in heaven"* or *"Life-giver in the light realms,"* and as we speak the truth, in the moment of invoking it, God's kingdom, God's light-realms, radiate through our spirits afresh, like a great flare bursting in the night sky, flooding with light the dark landscape. We'd grown used to the murkiness. But now, God's flare shows it as it is. We'd grown numb, perhaps, to the cries and the hurts around us, but now God's Fatherhood, God as our live-giver, brings them into our heart again. It's not anything our minds have to accomplish: but God's Word, through whom all things are made, in the praying re-makes us. Listen:

> *Give us thy food for the coming day* (*Give us this day our daily bread*).

We're not asking God to provide breakfast for us. His Word reminds us we receive everything from God: our upbringing, our nation, our destiny, the air we breathe, eyes, brains — the ability to earn our breakfast — all out of God. The praying recreates us afresh into our true selves as his grateful children.

And God's good trustees. Because just as, even if you're alone, you never pray "My Father," in that he's Father of us all, so you never pray

"Give me…my food." We know, it's for the family. The prayer recreates us kinfolk who share. That's his kingdom coming in our world!

Someone said, "Prayer is to implore God, not impress people." Well taken. But think about "im-press." A press transforms a blob of ink into a pattern of images on paper. So true prayer, deriving from God's heart, does im-press you who pray it, into the shape of God's heart. You can't then be selfish or racist or godless: it would be against nature. Suppose, after the Lord's Prayer, you then go on to pray, "Lord, comfort that lonely old man down the street:" God having re-shaped your compassion into his, you'll now go with God to bless that lonely old man yourself. Praying for those who hurt, even tearfully, but without trying to heal what hurts them, is not prayer, but pious chatter.

When we pray life-changing, life-affirming, life-empowering prayer, we are God's instruments. Given our vocation of service and shown how to live it, we're held responsible for doing so. Humbly, though. We're not God. Our morning prayer makes that plain:

Forgive our transgressions, even as we forgive our transgressors.

As you say it, you're a person who needs forgiveness; and you're a person who forgives. Accepted just as you are, you accept your brothers and sisters just as they are, your words and life dovetailing afresh. And moving your prayer to its summit:

Bring us not to the test, but deliver us from the opposing powers.

The culminating liberation! We're not controlled by our genes, or our peers, or society's ills. Even in temptation, we can trust God whose strength empowers. And our prayer, deep to deep, and open to the "Yes!" of the God who creates all things new, now recreates us new in the praying of it and lifts us to the top of our potential.

So we can move out of the praying into the thick of the battle alongside God to make life less dirty, less inhumane; to struggle for values, sanity, happiness; to insist that what's done in our homes, the media, the legislatures, is caring and right. When we get up from our knees ahead of us are days filled with crucial engagement, side by side with the living God.

And with this difference, that now we know:

*Of thee are the realms, and the energies, and the radiances
Throughout the life cycles, eternally, forever.*

What could more transform one's life? What could better bring "*the Kingdom, and the power, and the glory*? This shall be God's world.

Pray it true. Live it out. And it shall be.

Chapter 8: God's detours

Mark 5:21-34

And a great crowd followed him and thronged about him. And there was a woman who had had a flow of blood for twelve years, and who had suffered much under many physicians, and had spent all she had, and was no better but rather grew worse. She had heard about the reports about Jesus, and came up behind him in the crowd and touched his garment. For she said, "If I touch even his garments, I shall be made well." And immediately the hemorrhage ceased; and she felt in her body that she was healed of her disease. And Jesus, perceiving in himself that power had gone forth from him, immediately turned about in the crowd, and said, "Who touched my garments?" And his disciples said to him, "You see the crowd pressing around you, and yet you say, 'Who touched me?'" And he looked around to see who had done it. But the woman, knowing what had been done in her, came in fear and trembling and fell down before him, and told him the whole truth. And he said to her, "Daughter, your faith has made you well; go in peace, and be healed of your disease."

"The social program of the Volunteers of America was not planned in detail and inaugurated by national orders and directives. New programs were begun and new services offered as new community needs became evident."

It makes sense. This national strategy is a determined policy of local flexibility. Volunteers are commissioned, trained, and expected to be sensitive to the needs of local people, and each local ministry devises its own variety of programs to meet them. So across the nation there's as much diversity as commonality.

Historically, though, this was not an inevitable strategy. In the Salvation Army, from whom Volunteers of America separated in 1896, operations were directed from London. A politically-minded commentator or a skeptic, might hazard that this new insistence on local autonomy was part of the nationalistic climate which stimulated the break from English supervision. A pragmatist might say it works. I'd like to offer the thought that the Booths and their co-founders shaped this policy out of a deep response to the ministry of Christ.

Clearly, they were people of great faith, deeply versed in the Scriptures, their motivation Christ's life and ministry. They were firm that the social work never be pushed to the detriment of the spiritual. It was because of the physical needs of "the poorer folk, the unfortunate and friendless" that the social program came into being. But it was always based on their spiritual needs. Maud Booth insisted that the Volunteers of America "was founded as a soul-reaching, soul-saving Organization," and Ballington wrote,

> *Paramount in importance...far above the feeding of the body, the housing of the poor, or (their) uplifting with physical hands, is the spiritual work. Whatever else wanes or weakens, let not this branch of the work (be) lacking. In our efforts to...bring them material benefits, there should underlie, like sure, deep, ever-running current, the spiritual well-being, the saving of the heart.*

On the other hand, he knew "you cannot talk to a man about God when he is hungry and half-clothed. You have to feed and clothe him first." Indeed, a person suffering any one of the anguishing variety of hurts afflicting humanity, was not first talked to about God. First the Volunteers tried to ease the suffering. The long tradition is of "prompt and effective action in time of emergency." It was "God's Ambulance Corps!"

The flexibility the founders devised seems theologically sound. Consider our text. It seems to tell of an hour in Jesus' life which was one switch after another. A crowd gathered to hear him. He was about to begin when a man named Jairus, who had a dying child, pleaded for help. Whatever his plan for the day had been, we infer from Mark it did not include a journey to Jairus' house. But Jesus went with him. On the way, a woman in the crowd who "had a flow of blood for twelve years," needed his help and again interrupted him. Once more, he deferred what he was doing, and attended to her.

This was typical. His family, his friends, those who hated him and those who needed him disturbed his meals, detoured his journeys, diverted his teaching and distracted his thoughts right on to Golgotha. There the jeers of some and the needs of others interrupted his dying. His last troubler was a thief. Always, he was open to interruption.

Should we copy him then? Can we? When someone's need radically switches our day around, can we imitate Christ and learn how to get through it? Can we adopt his art of meeting those whose needs frustrate our plans, with a grace that works? It would certainly lift the spirits of those we are trying to help, our own morale, and actual remedial results.

In what Jesus did — letting this woman's illness override what he'd intended to do — he clearly showed that to him, human beings are more important than plans. The trouble with plans is they tend to set hard, like a crust, even over our feelings. So when people unexpectedly plead with us about their plight, if we could let their need break through the crust, we'd find that helping them not only eases their problem, but that our resulting relationship with them means more to us than any plan. Instead of nuisances, they become part of our lives.

Now Jesus obviously didn't simply give in to everyone. That would be to surrender his own personhood, which is as wrong as denying it in others. No, he would always weigh and consider how much, or how best to help. He always treated people as full human beings. That's Jesus of Nazareth, and that's Volunteer policy. Even, theology.

Here's another possibility. Someone whose need calls you to stop what you're doing and help them may enable you to be what God wants you to be. At its best, life is for sharing the world in active love. Now quite unexpectedly, you're given a chance to do just that, which otherwise you wouldn't have.

A while ago, Renee and I were in England, staying with my sister Phyllis and her daughter Kerry. The vacation was tragically interrupted when Kerry swiftly developed a fatal illness. She was 30, Phyll's only daughter. There are four older sons. In weeks, death closed around Kerry's paralyzed little body. She needed tender and total care. She wanted to die at home, among the family. Nurses came three times a day, the doctor every day. But it was Phyllis who was her ministering angel. Every night, Kerry's four brothers took turns to be her gentle nurses. They were different men, now, from those we'd known before, and perhaps from those they'd known themselves. And Kerry herself was a heroine. She kept her sense of humor; the sweetest, bravest young lady one could ever meet.

Kerry died, and our hearts were broken. But she helped her mother and her brothers reach their potential as human beings. They lived out, and lived up to, what I know as Christ-love. Those whose pleas switch our plans may be giving us the opportunity to be what we were put on earth for.

It may work like this. If you allow someone's plight to interfere with your plans, you may be letting God's Spirit into your life. You say, "Here's someone whose distress makes me detour round what I was doing. Then I will trust God to meet me in the detour." It may well be the detour is actually God's plan for your day, as well as God's plan for your hinderer's day.

Let me offer an instance. Imagine us back in 1957, Renee and I and our three children, contented Britons, mortgage paid, in England's most delightful county; good churchpeople, I, indeed, a lay preacher. Weekdays, I was a Government inspector, on a sure career ladder. Then one drizzling Sunday night, driving to lead worship, my headlights picked out in the rain a man huddled at a bus stop. He must either be a stranger or an idiot, because buses didn't run in Cornwall on Sunday nights. So I stopped. He had a foreign accent. American, I guessed. He was trying to get to a country church. If I drove fast I would just have time to take him there before my service began. He was the Rev. Joe Rosemurgy, First Methodist Church, Newark, Ohio. In the days that followed, he came to a service or two I conducted. Then, back in Ohio, he told his Bishop, Hazen G. Werner, who thereupon invited us to the U.S. ministry. Talk about an interruption!

But praying that the Holy Spirit was in this, we took the detour and resigned the sure career ladder. We sold all we owned, bade farewell to loved ones and made the venture of faith. Our hope ever since has been that this was God's will.

What's much more important to Volunteers of America is the designed openness of the founders to interruptions and detours. It was the *modus operandi* from the beginning, from the top to the farthest, smallest unit, taken-for-granted. Even before 1896, Ballington was devising innovative programs for immigrants who couldn't speak English. In response to local needs, rescue homes for women were established and staffed, relief projects inaugurated to meet emergencies. There were innumerable forms of social relief work devised "in every case...in response to a community need." Typically, it was an interruption which caused Maud Booth to start what became her life's great work. Remember the letter from a prisoner in Sing Sing, asking for help? The result was a ministry which over her 52 years aided tens of thousands of prisoners and their families. What characterized the Volunteers of America were Spirit-filled detours!

Certainly, that's what characterizes the account we read. For Jairus, for the woman in the crowd, and for Jesus, these were unplanned encounters. Surely the Holy Spirit was in every one. And surely the gracious will of the Father was exhilaratingly done in each that day.

So, is that it? Should I now write, "Go and do thou likewise," and you respond, "Amen, we will!"? Could you now go off in your Volunteer car, or to your Volunteer desk, confident you'll imitate Christ in this? As you handle those whose needs urge sudden infuriating changes on you, or require violent detours of program or plan, will you be unconditionally Christ-like?

Then listen to one thing more: the Gospel. Up to this, we've been reaching toward the Gospel, approaching the beginnings of the Gospel. Now, let us come to its heart. The Gospel has to do with our empowerment, with our being made able. As we let the Holy Spirit lead each of us individually and as an organization to Jesus the Christ, he will empower us to do the loving will of God our Father. This is the Gospel.

Let's see ourselves in the first place not as those who try to copy Christ in helping people, but as what we are in the first place, people who ourselves need Christ's help.

Listen: "There was a woman in the crowd..." Let's see her, not as an incidental character in an ancient story, but as a living human being. She may be more like us than we thought, which is why the Word of God confronts us with her.

This woman in the crowd has no right to be in the crowd at all. According to the law of her people, a woman in her condition must keep apart from society all the days she suffers it. The Book of Leviticus sets it out, and everyone around her knows it. By Hebrew law, anyone who touches her — her husband, her children, strangers in the crowd — is thereby socially and religiously "unclean." She has no place out among people. She has no place in God's house. She has only a restricted place in her own home, as a mother and as a wife. For twelve years, it's been so.

The law laid it down that a woman breaking certain of these rules shall be killed. Now feel her predicament. Going out in the crowd to get help means she has to keep her condition to herself. She is living under the secret shadow of death. This has to do with hidden uncleanness, a very private sense of guilt and the shadow of death.

Am I not talking of things that concern you? None of us under the pure light of God would be found perfectly clean, would we? We have things in our personality, our past, our habits, our character, which spoil our lives and the lives of others. Moreover, being human means I'm a man walking toward death, writing to people who will die. The Word of God does touch our condition.

"She has suffered much, under many physicians, and has spent all that she had, but is no better, but rather grows worse." She has turned for help to every source that promised it. But none could. Now all her money is gone. Cures are never free, and when you have nothing in this world, you've reached the end of your tether. What can you do?

"She has heard the reports about Jesus," and comes to him. Even though she turns to him only as a last resort, he accepts her.

Desperate, she touches his garment as if there is healing in his robe. There are many things in the life of faith we can't fully comprehend, and respond to only within the limits of our understanding. So with her. She touches his garment. The Church has believed that he honored even this child-like faith. Her body, responding to his acceptance of her as a person, healed. And I believe it.

But Christ came into the world not to heal bodies. He came to save people, to make every aspect of life whole. "Save" comes from the Latin *salus*, to heal; "whole," has the same root as "holy." See it now: "saving" is "healing," which is "wholeness," which is "holiness." Christ came to heal each person's body, mind, emotions, soul, the whole person. This is why the Holy Spirit draws us to Christ, to make every aspect of our lives whole and holy.

And this is why the woman is not through. Not yet! She's healed in her body, but Jesus will help her more than that. She wanted physical help, but that's not enough for him. She is a whole person to him, and he must heal her totally — wholly! "Who touched my garment?" he asks. The woman comes forward. She's tried to hide herself in the throng. But he knows each of us, even in a crowd.

Now she can admit the truth, glad someone cares enough to hear her out. And he says to her, "Daughter, your faith has made you well: go in peace." And it's over. Twelve long years of inability to be the person she was meant to be. Over. Now, she can fulfill her life. Now she is a woman, she is a whole human being! And the account ends.

But not the empowerment. For there's one thing more: the price. Cures are never free. This woman has nothing with which to pay. But there is a cost; and someone has to pay it. So Jesus pays it himself: the Scripture says, "Something had gone out of him." When he helped anyone, he was using himself up. It was always so. He was not just giving them help. He was giving them himself. Those who've been helped by him have part of him in them now. They have his spontaneous and unselfish love in them now. Christ-love.

At the last, as you know, he gave himself utterly, on a cross — for me, I believe, and for mortal people like me who are badly in need of help: fathers, mothers, sons, and daughters; with uncleanness about us and nothing with which we can pay. Ours, too, is a story about an issue of blood; for it was by a flow of blood from his body that we are healed.

If you'll let him do so for you, part of him comes into you, his immediate and unconditional love. So that you, who perhaps unexpectedly touched his garment in this reading of the Word, now detour round what you'd planned and do what you were put on earth for. Attend with grace and love to those who need you.

It leads to health in its full sense of wholeness. It's the faith that makes you well, you and yours. Let the gracious Spirit lead us to touch the Son's garment, that each of us, love-filled, will go out to serve… with no interruptions!

Chapter 9: A hard question yields to the great vocation

From John 9:1-7

> *As Jesus passed by, he saw a man blind from birth. And the disciples asked him, "Rabbi, who sinned, this man or his parents, that he was born blind?" Jesus answered, "It was not that this man sinned, or his parents, but that the works of God might be made manifest in him."*
>
> *"We must work the works of him who sent me, while it is day; night comes, when no one can work. As long as I am in the world, I am the light of the world." As he said this, he spat on the ground and made clay of the spittle, and anointed the man's eyes with the clay, saying to him, "Go, wash in the pool of Siloam..." So he went and washed, and came back seeing.*

How can a loving God allow such suffering? It's the most difficult question in my heart, and in yours probably. It can't either be ignored or manipulated, we're all too close to it. There's never been a good answer. And here's an added question for us whose vocation is helping people. Are we spending our days trying to ameliorate the very pain God permits?

Some of humanity's good minds have struggled with it. Euripedes asked it long ago: Do the gods indeed rule over us, or are we the sport of chance? John Milton wrote *Paradise Lost* trying to "justify the ways of God to man." Dostoevsky struggled life long in the quest; it never left him alone. Our time's wise C.S. Lewis strove manfully with it. But no answers satisfy us. We want to know what justice there might be in God's creation, what meaning in the cruel confusion of so much hurt. Something in us refuses to give up.

It might help to start at the beginning. The Bible says God created the world good, all nature healthy, man and woman its happy custodians, harmonious with each other and the environment. But eons followed in which people misused nature and each other, acted from self, anger and other base motivations, chose wrong means for wrong ends. In short, we spoiled things. It's gone on endlessly, and still does. Ordered nature became disordered, right relationships wrong, formed health deformed. And life deteriorated from the bliss of Eden to the misery of a billion victims. So among our legacies now are uncountable varieties of evil, innumerable diseases of mind and body. That's our situation.

But does it help us figure out, say, God's role in the Holocaust? First, then, let's clear away some obvious and less searing facts.

Some pain is essential: we couldn't live without it. You fill your bath, and before sitting down, dip your toe in. If it's scalding, your toe will scream. That's helpful. If you sit down anyway, you'll get what's coming to you. A lot of the world's pain happens because we break natural laws. It's "deserved." Paul spoke an iron truth: "Don't be deceived… what a man sows, he'll reap" (Gal 6:7).

Probably most of the pain of the human race is caused by the human race. It's part of that precious and dangerous gift, our liberty. Perhaps we could have been created moral robots. Even now, God could stop people from harming each other and themselves. But God doesn't. A believer's task is not to wish for divine interference in human choices, but to try making Godly choices.

For we are clear about this: God doesn't cause suffering. Destroying people's minds, or crippling their bodies is not God's will. It's a lie to call an "act of God" an epidemic that devastates, a storm that downs a plane. It's to accuse God of being a fiend. Good parents don't do that to their children. Is God less loving than a good parent?

The people who know this best are those who, even out of deep distress, will nevertheless tell you, "God's been good to me, and helps me every moment." Good life is the will of God. Sanity, health, peace are the will of God. When doctors innovate and heal and care, they're not frustrating God's will, but carrying out a loving purpose. Their minds and hearts are meant for this. Whether therapy comes from medicine, surgery, prayer, or some laws of life we don't yet understand, healing is of God.

But all this is only to clear the ground for the crux of the question: "Why, if there's a good God, do the innocent suffer?" Granted, some pain is helpful, some earned, and most man-made, we're still left with the terrible question, "Why does such overwhelming hurt happen to those who don't deserve it?" Human faces covered with flies, abused babies, a young mother with cancer: as Paul wrote (Rom 8:22), "the whole creation groans in travail together." Why do the innocent suffer?

Perhaps it's helpful what Jesus said about motherhood: "When a woman is in travail she knows sorrow, but when she is delivered of the child, she no longer remembers the anguish for joy" (John 16:21). Can good things be born out of suffering? It's certainly been a wonder to me, as I've met people of different experiences and backgrounds, that so often the finest folk are those who've anguished. The fires of suffering do refine the dross out of a person and leave the gold.

Can there be value to suffering? The poet John Keats called it "the valley of soul-making." And he knew! As a boy, he and his only brother saw their mother through terminal tuberculosis. In those days T.B. was considered not only deadly, but fearfully contagious, such that all belongings of a tubercular corpse had to be immediately piled outside and incinerated. The boys saw her buried, and everything she'd touched, burned. Keats grew to manhood, his life devoted to poetry. His brother, who was now all he had, began coughing blood. Keats cared for him, buried him, and put his belongings on a bonfire. And then his own coughing told him he soon would die. But in the little while left him, in a small room in Italy, he wrote glorious poetry. Good things are born out of pain.

Paul believed so. Look what he became and look what he did! He was able to say (Rom.5:3), "Tribulation produces endurance, and endurance, character, and character, hope!"

Here's another truth we might take from Jesus. In the long human story, suffering need not go for nothing. Perhaps those unnumbered generations of human wrongness have accumulated a huge burden, which some of us inherit pieces of, in mind or body. And which we bear, then, for the human family's sake? It's helping our kindred carry the load? Hold on: it's not for nothing you suffer! It's not without meaning: it's for the family. And know this. Your Lord did it before you. He accepted our sorrows, took on our wounds; and when the hammers thudded home the nails, he didn't rebel though he was innocent. He was doing it for the family.

Perhaps God does not explain the dark mystery of it all here to those who are comfortable and strong, but does explain it, in good time, and in a way too deep for words, to those who suffer and still hold on, work on, trusting. We live in the incomplete. Faith is not knowing, but taking the word of One who does. Jesus assures us that God doesn't look at life as we do, or at death as the end of it. But that our time here somehow trains us for the experience to come. Does temporary pain — and all pain here is temporary — have an eternal value?

Recall Jesus telling of the starving beggar named Lazarus, whose days were one long cry of pain (Mk. 16). When death came to him, Jesus said, his lifetime of misery had prepared him for the near presence of God. Jesus is not fobbing us off with "pie-in-the-sky-when-you-die." There is justice in heaven.

Meantime, we do have enough light to live by. We are moving toward full clarity. Paul said (1 Cor. 13), "Now, we look through a glass, darkly: but then, face to face. Now I know in part; then, I shall understand fully, even as I have been fully understood." And this, all in the context of the gifts which God gives us, of faith, hope, and love, and of which the greatest is a love that "bears all things, believes all things, hopes all things, endures all things" and never ends! It was enough for Jesus, who in his own worst hour said, "Father, into thy hands I commend my spirit."

But surely there is more we can learn? I want to turn to what Jesus brought to the problem in the account from John with which we began. As the disciples and Jesus pass by a man blind from birth, the disciples ask, "Rabbi, who sinned, this man or his parents, that he was born blind?" If God is all-loving and all powerful, why was the man born blind? He's innocent as any, but born to darkness and humiliation. "Why should this innocent man suffer so?" The disciples want to do what we've been doing, struggle with this hard, hard question. But Jesus doesn't. He won't. Instead, he goes to the man, and helps him! That's his teaching. Help the man. Now. While there's still light! Jesus said we pass from our lives, and one another's, so quickly. So "what can I do to help — now?"

Let me share an instance of what seemed surely to be Jesus, helping now. Where I was a pastor in New Jersey, our congregation had a little seven-year old boy named Glenn Garvett. One day, as he was cycling with his father and sister, the boy suddenly died. His father Tom was overwhelmed, probably with anger. He just couldn't understand what God was doing. And Tom wrote down his pain, raging against God. It was printed in Glenn's funeral bulletin. You can feel Tom's pen stabbing against the page, from his heart. But you can also sense a gentle Lord helping him even in his rage. Listen:

> *How many times must I relive the bitter experience,*
> *In depths of night or as I gaze from the window on the spot*
> *On which he fell? Three riders in a line:*
> *Father, daughter and son descending downhill to the park*
> *And brook beyond. Then, final words, "Dad, wait for me."*
> *And life became robbed of its innocence.*
> *White uniforms, blue uniforms blur by, red flashing lights,*
> *And a boy's body... Justice, mercy, and love: these have been*
> *Your names to me, God! Where were you, then?*
>
> *Couldn't you in your infinite wisdom find another way*
> *To achieve your purpose,*
> *And let a healthy, happy seven-year old boy live?*
> *Did you know him as we knew him? High up in the house,*
> *In his room, his questions, habits and life-thoughts*
> *Crowd my mind. From here, we saw trees and sky,*
> *And talked of seasons and of stars.*

We spun a globe and dreamed of journeys
We would make together, some day.
Here, after the lamp was snapped off, we talked,
Illuminated by the soft night-light in the hall
And by our love for each other;
And hugged and kissed goodnight.

Did you know how meticulous he was?
How careful of his things — and of yours?

Hear me, God!

He loved the morning birds and the sunlight on the clouds.
He cautioned his father to rake winter leaves softly
So as not to break the crocus, daffodils or hyacinths
That lay beneath: a young man giving fresh new life
A chance to live. — Couldn't you have done the same?

Make no mistake, Glenn was a boy! He ran and played hard,
Was a devoted friend who enjoyed life to the full —
Like always asking for a second helping of home-made pie.
What kind of man would he have grown into — life unfulfilled?

God, in my reasoned emotion, I want to smash my fist
Through brick or board in defiance of this utter futility.
News of his tragic death spread quickly,
And the human response was immediate:
Arms and spirits joined together to uphold,
And the upholders to be upheld. Darkness could not conceal

The grief that tossed in heart and mind
On beds of despair that night.
In a shocking instant, this boy became every boy!
Torrents of love sprung from human hearts —
Uplifting and sustaining.
All differences that would be defended in other days,
Melted away as folk became one, in a common life-purpose:
Compassion.

We loved our son with boundless love. But, if we had held him

On the eve of his departure into the greater life
Until our arms ached, we could never be as close to him
As we are now. His soul has been breathed into ours,
Engraved upon our hearts and minds as never before...
To be carried by us into eternity.

It changed the course of all our lives: bitterness and apathy
Gave way for one glowing instant before the onslaught of love.
Life is short, whether we live to seven or seventy.
For our lights, too, will someday sputter and die.
Live each day to the fullest, as he did:
With the same trust and joy!

...Sermons said, hymns sung, are stone,
Compared to human love-giving. — Meaningless words?
Unless...we hold each other with the same love
We held that small body that slid to earth,
One spring afternoon. Is this your purpose, oh God?
Acceptable to each of us, for our time?
Good night, sweet prince, my darling son.
Your life shall be mine forever more. Amen.

His Lord was surely with this father as he struggled to understand, helping him open his heart to grace, so that from then on he could live with trust again, so he could know, deeply, that though now we do see in a mirror dimly — "then, face to face." For God's promise of love for ever, and never closer than in the presence of death, is throughout his Word.

I was 15, and in a World War II hospital when I first saw it. I had broken my nose playing rugby. Well, a lout of a fullback broke it. But I was now in a long ward with 30 other patients, some lightly ill like me, some seriously, all mixed together. The old man in the bed next to mine was dying of a tumor in the head. He was blind with it, and suffering terribly. But silently. I was too scared to look at him. It was Sunday evening, after a day of boredom for me, agony for this dying old man whom I could not look at.

Some church folk brought a harmonium and asked to worship with us. There were hymns, scripture, prayer, words of encouragement. Then I noticed the old man was trying to lift his hand to them, so I called out, and one came and leaned over the old chap. "Could we sing, 'Abide With Me,' sir?" "Surely, friend." A nod to the harmonium player, and the familiar tune began.

At first, only a few patients joined the church folk. Then we saw the old man trying hard to get the words out too. And we began to sing them with him, for him. A strange thing happened. Tears started down my 15-year-old face. Soon, most of us were weeping as we sang. There was great love in that ward. It was the first time I was conscious of God, in the room with me:

I fear no foe, with thee at hand to bless: ills have no weight, and tears no bitterness; where is death's sting? Where, grave, thy victory? I triumph still, if thou abide with me. Hold thou thy cross before my closing eyes? Shine through the gloom, and point me to the skies. Heaven's morning breaks and earth's vain shadows flee. In life, in death, Oh Lord, abide with me...

The old man died that night. He died well-prepared. And what grace filled that ward! I still feel it.

I was driving the highway recently and heard Dr. Bernie Seigel tell of six-year-old Jason Gould, who got cancer. When Jason was seven, he wrote a book titled, *My Book To Help Children Who Get Cansur*. When he was 11 he wrote another, called, *Now I Can Spell Cancer*, saying, "If God had wanted me to be a basketball player, he'd have made me seven feet tall; but he gave me cancer, so I can help people." Eleven-year-old theology, perhaps, but what radiant discipleship!

My close friend was Dr. Webb Pomeroy. We were going to retire together, and he would teach me to fish. But he caught a strange, incurable disease. In the hospital where he learned he was dying, he asked the chaplain to visit and be with him awhile. The chaplain suggested they pray, and Webb wanted to, asking, "What shall we pray for?" The chaplain said, "Let's pray for a miracle, that you'll be healed." Webb thought a bit, and answered, "Miracles are so rare. Let's pray for the little girl next door, that she'll get one. For me, let's pray that God will help me handle my illness well." Good things are born out of pain. Later, as Webb was preparing for death, came a prayer that was straight out of Jesus' Way: that God might make use of his suffering. He left his ravaged body to the hospital, so doctors afterwards could go on working for a cure. He was doing it for the human family. And it helped him.

Does this help solve this insoluble old question? Well, know this, you who anguish, or must watch those who do: there are qualities born in suffering which easy, shallow lives know little of. Suffering brings depths and breadths of soul which can't be obtained any other way. It's a way of facing it that Jesus himself found affirming: surely much of his Christliness was hammered out on the anvil of distress. If you choose to face suffering his way, you can become like him, and enter an unmatched fellowship both with the human family and with our Lord. Nothing can compare with that.

That is why Paul, following Christ up the dreadful path to execution, could affirm: "Who shall separate us from the love of Christ? Shall tribulation, or distress, or persecution, or famine, or nakedness, or peril, or sword?" No! "I am sure that neither death, nor life, nor angels...nor anything else in all creation, can separate us from the love of God" (Rom. 8:36). Know this, you who suffer: open yourself to him, and you'll experience the heart of God at a depth you couldn't have reached any other way.

How you respond to suffering is your decision. You can whimper, be bitter, and rebel. Or, you can work with God in it and force good out of it? That's what Paul meant. God works for good in all things, *with* those who love him. Good can come, but won't come on its own, and not by God's action alone, but as we work with God in it. Ballington Booth wrote in his New Testament, in the notes for his first sermon, alongside the words of Jesus which he'd heavily underlined, "Heal the sick, cleanse the lepers, raise the dead, cast out devils:

freely ye have received, freely give: God's operations often depend on man's cooperations."

Perhaps God has placed you near people in anguish for your sake, too, that you might develop into the person he wants you to be. Imperfect Peter, average John, and those other ordinary men had to confront leprosy and paralysis and mental horror until they themselves were changed into disciples: servants of God and of their fellows. That's what God wants of us: that we become disciples and choose to be Christ-people in our community. He'll one day ask us to account for the way we treated people who suffer.

It's true, then, that for the full answers to this old, hard question, we may have to wait until we get home, when God will explain to us. But meantime — it's miraculously enabling — learn from Jesus of Nazareth, you who suffer. Work with God in it, and it must come right in the end.

And you who do not suffer. Your community has many who do, some in their bodies, some in their minds, souls, hearts. Don't just ponder at a distance. Go to them, while there's still light. Be with them, help them, love them, lift them!

This is Christ's answer to our question. Let's live by it.

Chapter 10: Getting the message, at last

Matthew 23:13-15

> *(Jesus said) Woe to you, scribes and Pharisees, hypocrites! Because you shut the kingdom of heaven against men; for you neither enter yourselves, nor allow those who would enter to go in. Woe to you, scribes and Pharisees, hypocrites! For you traverse sea and land to make a single proselyte, and when he becomes a proselyte, you make him twice as much a child of hell as yourselves.*

Jesus' message to the scribes and Pharisees seems clear enough. You religious people don't live your religion. Apparently, they didn't get it. Over and over in clear words he lifted up the faith they shared in the God of compassion. Time and again, they rejected the message. And the messenger? He was crucified. They never got it.

The question is: Do we?

Let me begin on a lighter note. Well, years later it seems lighter. I was a young sailor aboard *H.M.S. Dauntless*. Ordinary Seaman Webb, lowest of the low. But I was training and hoping to be an officer. It meant always appearing to be brilliant, since competition was fierce. One morning I was quietly scrubbing the quarter-deck when to my dismay the captain appeared, gold-striped and awesome. Unobtrusively, I scrubbed my way behind a large gun, and bent to my mop. It was too late. He'd spotted me, clicked his fingers, brought me cowering before him, and barked an order. I was off like a shot, and ten yards away before I realized I'd no clue what he'd said!

Sounded like, "Sinalmaapa!" What kind of a message is that? Petrified, I cringed my way back: "Repeat, sir. Please, sir?" Amazed at such stupidity, he snarled the order again. Away I went again, like lightning. But ten yards off, ears still petrified — "What did he say? " "Sinalmaapa? " I couldn't even guess. Grovel back to him. Astounded, he picked me up by my jersey, and bellowed: "I WANT A SIGNALMAN AND A PAD, YOU BLITHERING TWIT!"

To give and get a message is like clapping hands and dancing the tango, it takes two. As with teaching, where nothing is taught unless someone learns, so with a message. Someone has to send it, and someone has to get it or not much has happened.

In our faith life, this is serious because Jesus conveyed the most urgent messages ever spoken or needing to be received. Thankfully, unlike my captain, Jesus speaks them with utter clarity.

Let me offer an example. There's an account in Matthew 15 of Jesus' plain-talk which challenges me not only to look at my own life, but identifies as crucial this matter of clear language. A Gentile woman begs Jesus' help for her insane daughter. He doesn't answer. The disciples try to send her away. And he calls her a dog. That's a hard word.

Let's go back to the beginning, that is, to the beginning of words. What was man's first task? In the new-created world, according to Genesis 2:19, God first commanded man to name the creatures. Then God watched "to see what he would call them." Maybe we shouldn't shrug this off as old legend. There may be truth in it we live by, for good or evil. It implies, if we mis-name things, life will not be the way God meant it to be.

And life is not the way God meant it to be. Across the earth, awful diseases blight human life, religious excess rips peoples apart, crime and drugs control the streets. Could we be mis-naming things? Could it be that from the harmonious beginning, over the innumerable generations, people misused the creatures, nature, and each other. And to justify their misuse, misnamed things, persuading themselves they were doing no wrong by calling evil thoughts good, ugly things lovely, unnatural acts natural?

Perhaps that's what the Tower of Babel was about. People named themselves "lords of the earth," and built their imperious tower to prove it. Their understanding of God's lordship, God's nature and God's ways all disintegrating, there was now confusion of language. And there was violence and abuse unending. So we inherit a history of mis-naming, a legacy of sickness and insanity and all the vices.

You'd think that faced with this terrible lesson of the past, we would take seriously Genesis 2:19 and start naming things truly in the present. We already do it for our children. They live in danger until we teach them the difference between "fire" and "pacifier," "liking" and "striking." They must name things properly or life is unmanageable, even unbearable. They can't be happy, may not even be healthy, until they do. You'd think we'd learn the lessons both of history and child-raising, for survival's sake. Instead, we twist new dishonesties into the language.

For example, what does the word "promiscuity" mean? The dictionary defines it as, "abnormal unchastity." But in the soaps, the movies, the entire popular culture, what's "normal" now is exercising your "sexual preferences" with "sexual partners." So unchastity is not abnormal. Abnormal is normal and the word "promiscuity" has no meaning. "Adultery" has no meaning, because fidelity to marriage vows is becoming irrelevant.

A recent newspaper column by Miss Manners pulls us two ways. It used to be that "manners" had to do with how people behave decently to one another. The question asked elicited advice about responsible sexual behavior, and how to ensure one's next sex partner takes the right precautions. A woman should ask; and if he isn't, send him to the all-night pharmacy. Is this really a matter of "manners?" Or is it mis-naming, and part of the confusion not just of language but of life, eroding the structures we depend on to protect the powerless and the young?

Certainly as we read and try to interpret the Scriptures, true naming becomes an awe-filled task. We don't hope to be original or clever. Everything we think has been thought before, everything we say was said before, and probably better. The task is to name honestly. Out of the pure Word of God, to try to use words faithfully, about God about people, about their relationships. We must give right names to the problems of our time, and witness to their grace-filled solutions. When we speak faithfully of the true Word, there are opened Christ's possibilities of wholeness.

Because we believe of Jesus, "In the beginning was the Word...All things were made through him...And the Word became flesh, and dwelt among us, full of grace and truth" (John 1). He speaks truly and graciously God's thoughts, names as God names. When he properly names even sick aspects of our lives, we may return to health, sanity, and joy.

So, to return to our hard passage of Scripture. A Gentile woman pleads with Jesus for a healing in her family. He doesn't answer. She persists. The disciples urge him to send her away. He agrees. Still, she perseveres; and at last, he says to her: "It isn't right to throw the children's bread to the dogs." Dogs? Could that possibly be a correct name for her kind?

Let's be clear. In the Bible, if a person was called a dog, it was no compliment. It probably carried the same insult as when an American calls a lady a female dog, or a man the male offspring of one. What first upset Goliath — before the fatal pebble — was that David was treating him "like a dog." Samuel called his adversaries "dead dogs;" Isaiah derided his as "dumb dogs" or "greedy dogs." One of the nastiest curses an Israelite could lay on another (see 1 Kings 14:11) was that "dogs will eat your body." And it's Proverbs 26:11 which compares a fool who repeats his error to a dog who returns to his vomit.

We're thought of as dog lovers, but our literature is just as anti-dog. What annoyed Shylock was that his persecutors called him a dog. Hear the contempt of "yes-men" in Alexander Pope's couplet, engraved on the jeweled collar of a coddled canine: "I am his Highness' dog at Kew. Pray tell me, Sir, whose dog are you?"

It comes out in our slang, too. Some people and things are as "crooked" as a dog's hind leg. We speak of "dog days," "hang dog" expressions, "dog-eared." A "dogface" in the U.S. Army, like a Royal Navy Ordinary Seaman, is the lowest of the low and one who may spend time in the "dog house."

Jesus calls this woman "one of the dogs." Some kindly preachers who want to think of Jesus as always kind, have said he must have meant "puppies." But this is to miss the healing. The Gospel requires us to look at ourselves honestly in the mirror Jesus holds before our faces, and admit to what we see there. Therein begins the healing.

So we are to hear this Word of God as spoken to us.

Some time ago, I conducted the funeral of a man who put a pistol in his mouth and blew his head out. After a while, his widow could sit and tell me how it happened, and the picture emerged of two ordinary married people, neither of them vicious or unsound, gradually over the months, eating each others' hearts out: "dogs eating dogs." We're all capable of that. Many of us do it, over the years, to people at work, or to an offspring or our spouse? Be honest. There may be healing in it. Is it only other folk who've "gone to the dogs" ethically? Be honest. There may be healing in it.

That's what the hard Scripture about dogs can do — heal. Suppose we could face a truth about ourselves, as our Lord wants us to? Couldn't there be the possibility of healing for us, too? This woman shows the way. She so wants a healing in her family that she accepts humiliating truth about herself, not indignantly but cheerfully. So that Jesus is able to say to her, "Let it be as you desire."

So let's consider now three activities of our lives which need healing and which Christ addresses in order to heal us. First consider that account we read at the start about the religious people who were trying to entangle Jesus, wanting to trip him in the details of religion. He replied, "You hypocrites...you whitewashed tombs...you're children of hell!" That's major plain-talk. His message is that religious people are not to make sanctimonious display of religion but to live it. Whether they got the message or not, surely we're meant to. Hypocrisy is common. Certain male bower birds build high complex nests to attract their females. When they've mated, the female builds a small nest to raise her young, and the male carries on strutting round the nest he never lives in. Is that an analogy? Soren Kierkegaard said the philosopher Hegel built a magnificent philosophical palace for humankind, but himself lived in a shack alongside. Christians do the same. "No pious pretense, now: live your faith," says Jesus.

Here's a second plain message on what's thought of as "The Martha

Problem" (Luke 10:38). Mary and Martha were hosting Jesus in their home. Martha complained that her sister should be helping her, not hearing him. Again, Jesus didn't mince words. He told Martha that she was fussing over small things, whereas Mary was doing what was vital: hearing about God. Straight talk! Whether Martha got the message or not, we're surely meant to! That's what the Word is for, and does.

A third plain message in Mark (10:17-22) tells of a rich man who asked Jesus; "How can I enter eternal life?" Jesus put two probing questions to him, and cut directly to the core of his problem: "You want to know why you don't have eternal life? I'll tell you!" And he did. The man couldn't bring himself to give up his defect; so he could not enter that quality of life which lasts forever. He did get the message. It was downright blunt. Christ tells us frankly what we lack for eternal life.

So, Jesus speaks plainly and directly to heal us. But as we know, Jesus could also entrance people with moving stories. He shared through unforgettable parables the urgent messages of truth.

Take the problem of unlived religion. His direct accusations we may think are about someone else, so we don't get the message. But suppose he tells me a story of a man on the road to Jericho, stripped and beaten by thieves? Two religious people, one a minister, walk by on the other side, working on excuses. The man is finally cared for tenderly by a heathen, a Samaritan. Maybe now I will see myself in the story. Because I am a minister, and I'm not a heathen? Now, maybe, I'll get the message about living my religion. But there are two hypocrites in the story. Are you the other?

Or take the second problem, of our need to turn to God. If Jesus' direct advice didn't get through, because those Martha-type distractions are very possessive, then Jesus tells us a moving story about a Prodigal Son. Maybe now the truth can break in. Is that who I am? Is that what I'm doing with my life, wasting it in pig-like existence? But I can go back to my heavenly father. The possibility is, if we won't let the plain message in, perhaps it can get in a parable.

Why parables? Jesus' plain-talk, his many caring admonitions, obviously true explanations, even his strong moral warnings, may well be blocked by our layers of self-satisfaction. We may also be like a boy who does his math homework, by looking up the answers in the back of the book. If we're not involved in working out the problem, the right answer doesn't help a bit. In matters of faith, knowing the right answer isn't the point. If you can be moved in your whole self at a deeper level by Jesus' parables, experiencing the same changes but with everything still open, you'll continue to grow. Christians long years in the faith say they so pull us into real-life situations that not just our brains, but our memories, emotions, our whole being, are caught up in the truth.

The math analogy points to another effect of the parables. "$2+2=4$" is not a subjective truth, affected by my emotions or attitudes, or personality. It's an objective truth which properly focuses attention on itself, and leads my thoughts away from me to the fact that $2+2=4$. But in matters which determine my being and non-being, I must myself be involved. Jesus' parables do that. They draw the entire me into a true piece of life, grasp my reason, and reach beyond and deeper than my reason to my self, heart and soul.

Our human language grew around the function of describing the describable: "naming the creatures." So we say something is true when the idea of it in our minds matches the external object it points to. But in faith, we're having to use language based on things we know, to describe what precisely we cannot know, and are beyond what we can know. Our bread-and-butter language conveys well the idea of bread and butter, but is totally inadequate to describe either God or our relation to God. Jesus' parables help us do that.

So Jesus speaks plainly to us, and in parables. But he heals us also through humor. When he met those whom his straight-talk turned off, or whom his parables didn't reach, sometimes his humor got the message home, by making them laugh at themselves. Of course, there's a problem with humor. It doesn't travel well. Some Americans, for example, think Brits don't even know what it is.

So it's possible we won't chuckle at the same stuff first century Palestinians did. But maybe Jesus' humor sometimes did bubble out with a crucial message?

Of course — *of course!* — while he saw one child diseased, one woman insane, one man lost, Jesus' heart and life were heavy, and utterly at their service. He was with them in their distress. But in trying to draw people to truth, sometimes his humor helped someone get the message.

The Bible does say, (Psalm 2:4), "He who sits in the heavens, laughs." Two distinguished theologians were bosom buddies in their young days, probably sharing some undistinguished escapades; one became my eminent Chaired Professor, the other my Bishop. At his consecration, the Bishop received from the Professor a cable: "This proves (a) there's a God, and (b) he's got a sense of humor." I think God liked that. A minister friend of mine was baptizing a three-year old, and at the solemn moment, and the sanctuary hushed, the child's voice piped, "You're hurting my bottom!" It wasn't only the congregation who smiled.

If we believe Jesus was transparent to God and a complete human being, can we allow him a sense of humor? One pictures the sticklers of his day as serious. For example, they had a religious law forbidding eggs laid on the Sabbath. How do you stop an egg? And don't you have to be a bit grim to miss the rule's silliness. How could Jesus get people to see not only how silly it is but that it blocks the believer from a faith that matters?

So, Jesus asks you to recall the last time you whispered confidentially, "Hear about so-and-so? I mean...that thing in his eye? A speck! It's a real speck!" And Jesus says, "And you know what's in yours? A thirty foot log!" Get the message?

Here's a man taking a drink, but worried he might get a gnat in it. Laboriously he sets up a great contraption of muslin cloths to strain out any gnat. In all the palaver about gnats, he doesn't notice that he's actually swallowing a camel: walloping feet, four great knees, hump, rump, floppy body. And him so proud of the gnat he may have strained out! Surely even they would laugh? So now Jesus can make his point about our preferring trivia to the core of life, which is that we turn to God.

Jesus promises to give us a new self. More than that, he promises to give us himself. His heart will be our heart; his longings, our longings; his life, our life. He not only taught that this faith and true life are one, he lived it. Forgiveness? So many times, wholeheartedly, he forgave. Prayer? All night long, sometimes. The leader as servant? He took the towel to wash dirty feet. He didn't just believe in caring for the despised, he was their companion, went home and ate with them, loved them. He lived the message.

And it was cross-shaped. All we know of our Lord goes down into the depths of us: his deeds, words, everything he was, moves us in our profoundest being. And then, he bears us to the heights. His life lifts us. Such that ours become lifting lives, too: to the very top of human potential and joy! And at the last, there are his arms, outstretched on the cross for us! That our arms may stretch out to others; and we find that ours are empowered to serve, too.

So if you don't get it when he makes you laugh at the silly, godless things by which you block true life; if you don't get it from the inbreaking parables he shares with you; or even when he gives it to you straight, then hear it in his life, in its truth and compassion! See it in his cross-shaped service, come to fulfillment on Calvary, giving himself for you, that you might live in God, now and always, life and soul, and so give yourself for others.

Perhaps the words of Isaac Watts say it for us as well as any:

> *When I survey the wondrous cross*
> *On which the Prince of Glory died,*
> *My richest gain I count but loss,*
> *And pour contempt on all my pride.*

See, from his head, his hands, his feet,
Sorrow and love flow mingled down.
Did e'er such love and sorrow meet,
Or thorns compose so rich a crown?

Were the whole realm of nature mine,
That were an offering far too small:
Love so amazing, so divine,
Shall have my life, my soul, my all.

Chapter 11: How our daily grind becomes daily Grace

Matthew 25:14-30

(Jesus said) ... It will be as when a man going on a journey called his servants and entrusted to them his property; to one he gave five talents, to another two, to another one, to each according to his ability. Then he went away. He who had received the five talents went at once and traded with them; and he made five talents more. So too, he who had the two talents made two talents more. But he who had received the one talent, went and dug in the ground and hid his master's money. Now after a long time the master of those servants came and settled accounts with them. And he who had received the five talents came forward, bringing five talents more...His master said to him, "Well done, good and faithful servant; you have been faithful over a little, I will set you over much; enter into the joy of your master." And he who had the two talents came forward...(and is similarly praised and promoted). He also who had received the one talent came forward, saying, "Master, I knew you to be a hard man, reaping where you did not sow, and gathering where you did not winnow; so I was afraid, and I went and hid your talent in the ground. Here you have what is yours." But his master answered him, "You wicked and slothful servant! You knew that I reaped where I have not sowed, and gather where I have not winnowed? Then you ought to have invested my money with the bankers, and at my coming I should have received what was my own with interest. So take the talent from him, and give it to him who has the ten talents. For to every one who has will more be given, and he will have abundance; but from him who has not, even that which he has will be taken away. And cast the worthless servant into the outer darkness; there men will weep and gnash their teeth.

Jesus' final parable in Matthew is a story about work.

I was born in Wales. In my time, it was a little country where peoples' work lives were exploited for coal. After four terrible years as a frontline soldier in World War I, and although he was a skilled carpenter, my father could get work only as a miner. Deep underground, sometimes in a two-foot shaft, on his side in water, he worked ten-hour shifts by the flicker of a helmet-lamp for six pennies a ton. The absentee owner, a Lady Somebody in London who'd inherited the mine but never saw it, got twelve pennies a ton. You think I'm not interested in what Jesus said about work conditions?

Dad was not just a carpenter, but a craftsman. He made beautiful things. He was determined — and fortunate! — to finally escape the mines. But only for a job repairing the huge wooden rail road coal-wagons: all day with a five-pound hammer. You know what five pounds feels like, all day? When he was 50, the muscles in his shoulder stiffened and he couldn't raise his arm any more. But he'd done the work so his family could have a good home, and I a good education.

Much of the world's work is like that, underpaid, hard, unhealthy. Women with dulled eyes manipulate gidgets on a belt, children make cheap sneakers, or are used as prostitutes. All their lives they do work which ruins them. Yet here, we read of a basketball player advertising soft drinks for $40 million. We have questions about work.

Of course, Jesus' teaching is about more than work. This parable of a secular situation of his time illuminates spiritual reality of all times. It intersects our earthly life with our eternal life. A master going abroad calls his servants and entrusts his capital to them; to one he gives five talents, another two, another one. And he leaves the country. The man with one talent buries it. The other two put theirs to work, and do well. The master returns, and summons them for an accounting. The man who'd buried his talent Jesus calls "useless," who will now go into "the outer darkness." The two who had used their talents well are welcomed into their master's joy. What are we to learn from this?

First, that we're not to cozy up too quickly in life to the image of a distant but doting deity. The word is "master." We are God's servants. All of us.

Second, each is given "talents," gold coin in Jesus' time. It helps the parable for us that the word now means an ability to do something well. Everyone is given ability to do something well. Those who think they have none had better think again. Those with talents had better not regard them as their own achievement. They're a trust from God.

Third, our loans (of ability) vary one from another. We have different strengths and aptitudes. What we do have equally is the responsibility for using them.

Fourth, the master goes away. Having entrusted ability to each and placed us where it's needed, God then steps back and gives the world to our care.

Fifth, our work is vital not only to the world but to us. People who don't use their talents find themselves in what Jesus calls "the outer darkness."

Because sixth, one day the master returns, calls his servants to him and asks each, "What did you do with my trust?" It's an ultimate question.

At the level of our work lives, what light does this shed? It seems a stark assessment to many of us one-talent people. But it is meant to help us.

Let's look at another point in history. Consider the years when the first Volunteers of America began their work. Something certainly seems to have helped our predecessors! The early decades are striking not only for the staggering work burdens the Volunteers carried, but that they carried them so joyfully. Somehow, grace was at work in their grind. Wisbey's pages are as full of their prodigious output as their days must have been. They founded children's homes, hostels for working girls, shelters for homeless men, salvage depots, free hospitals, employment bureaus, wood-yards, salvage and rehabilitation centers. They gave emergency relief during tornadoes, explosions, and floods. They supplied coal, ice, milk and clothing to the poor, operated summer fresh-air camps for city children; helped men and women in prison and cared for their families. During the 1930s Depression they served nearly 25 million free meals. And all the while they carried out their full worship functions in mission churches and Sunday Schools. Incredible!

Though their load was heavy, their step was light. Service was a devotion, never dour. For example: in Chicago, in the founding year 1896, they took 10,000 poor children to a picnic. They fed them 14,000 lunches, 150 gallons of ice cream, 1,300 gallons of lemonade and cherry phosphate, and returned them home "with only minor casualties" (W. p. 55), perhaps including a stomach-ache or two? No grimness here. It was fun!

Ballington Booth typically would speak of "the light and joy of Christ" in life (W. p. 117). Wife Maud was of such blithe spirit, the prison inmates of her Volunteer Prison League chose as their motto, "Look Up and Hope" (W. p. 72). Gladness was integral and obvious. In Ballington's New Testament, after a plea to the finder to return the book if lost and found, he wrote "Here is only joy as we seek His pleasure." It's a joy deeper than happiness or satisfaction, though these can contribute. He lived "a Christianity with nothing that wearies — a Christianity that creates life, interest and energy" (p. 44). Perhaps it's akin to what those seventy in Luke 10:17 experienced: Jesus sent them out to serve people and they "returned again with joy." The Volunteers too, as their story shows, after extraordinary daily labors, returned home in the evenings with joy.

They believed their empowerment derived from their Lord. Somehow in Christ, work is both great and graceful. I'd like to approach how this may be by use of an analogy. Murray Kreiger in *A Window to Criticism* suggests how true poetry works. He gives this allegory: A wanderer comes upon a glass house filled with objects. At first, he peers into the house from the outside and is so attracted by the objects that he enters. The objects are replicas of the outside world, but made with artistry and skill. As he examines them, he keeps glancing out through the window-walls, comparing them with the real world outside. As he becomes more and more fascinated, he ceases to glance out the windows.

When finally he does look up, he sees with amazement that the windows have been transformed into mirrors and the objects in the house can now be seen in many reflections, from numerous angles and in varied lights. They are much more beautiful and perfect than the objects of the outside world. Indeed, they no longer appear to be replicas of what's outside, but the real things. It's a wondrous house!

Then another transformation takes place. The mirrors become windows again. But what the traveler sees through them is not what he saw before. The objects of the familiar world outside are now seen as shabby and distorted replicas of the true and lovely objects in the wondrous house. This continues to be so even when the traveler leaves the house.

And a final transformation takes place. The traveler determines that to make the world a fit place to live, he will spend his life trying to refashion the shabby objects of the world to be more like the vision he's seen in the wondrous house. And often he revisits it, to catch the vision again so it will not fade in him.

Might this allegory of the "wondrous house" help us to understand how Jesus' final teaching transforms work-lives? I suggest that being in Jesus' presence does for us all that the wondrous house does for the traveler. And more! Whereas the traveler of himself determines to try to refashion the world, when we come into Christ's presence we are empowered to refashion the world that it might become like the vision we've seen in Christ!

Consider in Luke 6, Christ's healing of the man "with the withered hand." It was his right hand, the one you shake hands with. His was a clump of bone and skin. So he couldn't offer it in a gesture of friendship to a fellow human being. He couldn't express love with it very well, couldn't stroke his wife's face with it, or his little girl's hair. In the aprocryphal Gospel to the Hebrews he says to Jesus, "I was a stonemason…I implore you, restore my hand." When he finds his hand healed, he can work again, take care of his family, help his community. He has his self respect. Everything changes for him. Christ is our "wondrous house."

Though Jesus' last teaching goes far beyond the matter of work to the lifting up of all human life, here and hereafter, even in the matter of work, we can glimpse the divine grace. Look at Jesus' hands. They're the hands of a workman. Mark 6 tells that when Jesus came from the desert back to his own village, many were astonished, saying, "Where did this man get all this? What mighty works are wrought by his hands! Is not this the carpenter?"

Perhaps what helped form his character were the hard years of work with his father. What Jesus did at the carpenter's bench from boyhood was for the family. It was therefore blessed. Certainly, when he was baptized in his thirtieth year, he had healed no one, taught no one. He had just made tables and ploughs. But John tells us God was "well pleased" with him. Can making a plough be as sacred as making a prayer? Maybe more, if it's a good plough, and a bad prayer. In Christ, one's faith shows on Monday as much as it did on Sunday.

When his ministry began, Jesus could extend hands callused from years of work and say with complete understanding, "Come to me, you who labor." And those who labored were lifted. So were those who were diseased or crippled or mentally ill. They found themselves clean and strong and whole. Children too would run to him. He would put a hand on each one's head and bless them. What must that have done for their future?

Consider the lepers Jesus healed. For example in Mark 1, he "sternly charged" a healed leper to tell no one. But to be a former leper, and keep it to oneself? Or consider the guests at the wedding feast in Cana. By Jesus' presence, the dull water of life was changed into excellent wine in their mouths. Consider the multitude who in Jesus' presence found their private stocks of loaves and fishes multiplying so all were filled.

Or when he turned his face to Calvary, see what happened to people there. Even on the road up, Jesus started the terrible journey carrying his cross, his body crippled by beating. The soldiers grabbed an onlooker named Simon, and made him carry the cross. Perhaps he didn't want to: most people seeing officials involved with criminals, stay out of it. But the Gospels speak Simon's name, and then his children's, as though they themselves became believers later on. Could it be that when Simon bent down, perhaps unwillingly, to put his shoulder under the cross, and looked into the bleeding face of the Man on the ground, something happened in his heart? When you come face to face with Christ, you start serving.

Or take the people on Calvary who gave Jesus that tranquilizing drink. All we know about them is that they saw his agony, and offered him drugged wine to ease his distress. A kind thought. Jesus refused it, perhaps wanting to meet this hour with clear eyes. But that's not the point. These people show what can happen when we look up to the Crucified One. We forget self and think of others.

There was another huddle of people on Calvary who were changed there. In the last months of Jesus' life, the Gospels show his family deserting him as a fanatic. But some came to his execution. They couldn't do much. But Jesus was grateful they found the love to be with him now. The worst about crucifixion was the torture to death. It broke the body. It also broke the heart. The custom was to crucify naked, and part of the horror was shame. Jesus had to suffer it. Except from this small group, who at his cross stood for him. That's the presence of Christ. You're able to stand for him. One might speak of the centurion, a hard man, at the top of a hard profession, who came to a truth on Calvary, "This was the Son of God." Death by crucifixion came partly by dehydration, which is an awful way to go: the only words Jesus spoke of his physical torment were, "I thirst." Someone heard, looked up at the cross, put a wet sponge on a lance, and touched his parched lips. Say what you like, it was a tender thing. In that crucifier, compassion was moved.

Or finally — for that day anyway — there was a thief who, dying with the Man of Nazareth, saw the difference. His were the last good words anyone said to Jesus. But they were words Jesus was longing to hear. He had promised, "I, if I be lifted up, will draw all men unto me!" And here Jesus was raised cruelly high on Calvary's tree. The first of millions who would look at Jesus there, wanted to change. When defeat seemed all round, and evil so evidently on top, a thief found new life: "Today, you will be with me in Paradise."

All this is open to us.

And more. Think of those who came into Christ's presence after Calvary. After the empty tomb — to the *risen* Christ! (Remember in his final teaching, how Jesus did spoke of a Master who returns?)

Mary Magdalene was the first, early on Easter morning. She came to embalm his corpse and met her living Lord. She ran to find the disciples. But they couldn't credit it yet. Then Cleopas and his friend, journeying silently home with their broken dreams, were joined by a third man, and felt their hearts glow. He broke bread with them, and they knew Whose presence they were in!

Now in the Upper Room, the disciples would meet the living Christ, know certainty, and find themselves able with power and joy to swing the door of life open for humanity.

Down through the pages of faith's history, time and again we see people coming into the presence of Christ and being *empowered* to spend their lives refashioning the world to be like the vision they've seen in Christ. Surely those first Volunteers of America were among them. They so entered the Master's presence that not only their own work-lives, but the work-lives of the people they served, moved toward joy.

We receive in Christ's presence a whole new way of seeing, being, deciding — and devoting our lives. It brings joy to us and in the work we do that lifts people. But now it becomes also our task so to re-create the working world of all the suffering ones that all are cared for, all can know as they work, they are indeed God's worthy people, with dignity they can celebrate; that their working ability comes as a responsible gift; that though there are not equal abilities, all have enough — and are equal in opportunities. And that at the accounting at day's end, and at the last there is a welcome into the Master's presence. "Come, share my joy!"

Chapter 12: The Age of the Spirit

Acts 3:1-11

> *Now Peter and John were going up to the temple at the hour of prayer... And a man lame from birth was being carried, whom they laid daily at that gate of the temple which is called Beautiful, to ask alms of those who entered the temple. Seeing Peter and John about to go into the temple, he asked for alms. And Peter directed his gaze at him with John, and said, "Look at us." And he fixed his attention upon them, expecting to receive something from them. But Peter said, "I have no silver and gold, but I give you what I have; in the name of Jesus Christ of Nazareth, walk." And he took him by the right hand and raised him up; and immediately, his feet and ankles were made strong. Leaping up he stood and walked, and entered the temple with them, walking and leaping and praising God. And all the people saw him walking and praising God, and recognized him as the one who sat for alms at the Beautiful Gate...and they were filled with wonder and amazement at what had happened to him.*

I said at the beginning that for me the heart of Christian faith is this: By grace, living in Christ shapes like a cross. As we stretch our arms wide like his to serve others, he leads us to the depth of God's compassion. And our whole being surges to a lifting life.

And this is so even after Calvary. Indeed, as our text shows, especially so. Up to now, we have experienced it in the Gospel accounts as we responded to what Jesus said and did. We were offered empowerment to our own compassionate service, cross-shaped and lifting. That power is, of course, still and always a mystery. We have spoken of it as grace, the gift of God's love poured out free and unmerited, enabling our own serving love. We have spoken of it as our Lord's presence, as in our depths we experience Jesus as God's Christ, and ourselves lifted to service.

After Christ's resurrection, the Divine Mystery who empowers us is more usually spoken of as the Spirit. This is no fresh or subsequent revelation or manifestation of God, of course. From the beginning of the Word in Genesis 1, with "the Spirit of God moving over the face of the waters" to Jesus' first announcement "The Spirit of the Lord is upon me" (Luke 4:18) and then on throughout the Gospels, the Divine Action is spoken of as the Spirit. But it is helpful to speak of the time since the conclusion of the Gospels as the "Age of the Spirit."

For a helpful summary of this chronology, we might again turn to Father Fred Kammer, who earlier guided us in the care of God's disadvantaged children, the *anawim*:

Stepping back to take the long view for a moment, theologians sometimes speak of salvation history as divided into three phases corresponding to the three-personed revelation of who God is. In other words, the Age of the Creator corresponds to the revelation of God living in the midst of the Hebrew people, passionately caring for them, and continually drawing them back to fidelity by the prophets and chosen ones.

The Age of Jesus comprises that very brief period in the life of Jesus of Nazareth reflected in the Gospels. The New Testament Jesus is seen through the eyes of faith as God breaking into human history, proclaiming the year of the Lord, reaching out to the anawim *of Yahweh, and profoundly identifying with them. Jesus passionately prophesies against those who would substitute the oppression of the law for the living kinship bond of Yahweh and Yahweh's people. Jesus calls God Abba ("Father") in a new revelation of intimacy with God. Then, in death and resurrection, Jesus seals this God's love for us in blood and testifies to "his way" as the definitive model for all of us as children of God. In a final movement, Father and Son together send the Spirit to the disciples to empower the continuation of the reign according to the pattern of Jesus Christ.*

The Age of the Spirit then spans human history from the powerful and charismatic first day of Pentecost to the end of time as we know it, when Jesus will come again as ultimate liberator. This age is about us and the presence and power of God in us. It is about now and this place, about billions of people struggling on one small planet for life and love, and the simple realities of personal journeys, families, work, birth, life, and death. Understanding the Spirit is about our lives.

So in the Age of the Spirit, on the voyage of faith this book charts, we turn to the account in Acts 3. The event in which Peter and John meet the lame beggar can be an exhilarating experience for us of the new age, can lift us into the life of the Spirit, ourselves "walking and leaping and praising God."

The account centers mainly on Peter and his faith. This is fitting for us since our voyage into the deep things of God began with Peter. Much has happened in his life since that first encounter with Jesus on the beach, including three shameful denials on the day of crucifixion. But no, he strides up the hill to the House of God filled with a quality he had never known. People would come to think of Peter as a saint. Here, he seems an ordinary man. Born of working-class parents, with a rough country boy's upbringing, scant education, few abilities, he was put to work young catching and selling fish. He grew to the limitations of one so raised, narrow, knowing little further than the end of his small town road. He was unreliable, perhaps cowardly. Jesus once called him by the worst name he ever used, "Satan."

Now he is a very different man, on his way up the hill to God's House. Just prior to this, he'd been part of that "Upper Room experience" described in Acts 2. The disciples, desolate at their Lord's death, had gathered to struggle with what had happened in their life with Jesus and what to do next. Prayerfully, they'd opened themselves to God. As they did, they felt the Holy Spirit powerfully present, lighting their hearts like fire. They saw their past with Christ filled with new meaning, the present incredibly potent, and their futures opening into the Kingdom of God. They realized in themselves, now, Jesus' promise. He had indeed come that they might have life, and have it abundantly. They determined to live it, at once!

So Peter had gone straight from that meeting, out to the crowd. With no training, in the country accents of a Galilean fish seller, he had witnessed with authority, his words illuminating them like light, the truth of what he was saying applying to their lives as if he were speaking their language! Many were changed that day through a man who had himself been changed by God's Spirit and was letting it course through him.

And now he's striding up the hill to the House of God. Why would he need to? Join others at worship I mean? Surely he has more of the Spirit in him than they do. Well they are his people, men and women who come together to worship, read the Scriptures, share one another's prayers, joys, troubles. That is where he must witness to Christ.

And as Peter walks to the House of God, a beggar sits at the door. That may be embarrassing for the worshippers because the word "worship" comes from "to serve," to serve God — but also, as God makes plain, to serve the *anawim*, the disadvantaged. Worshippers can easily forget them, and ignore what worship is, unless one of them is actually waiting at the entrance.

And the man asks for help.

Notice him. His only means of getting food is by begging. It demeans him. A beggar in body, he's become a beggar in mind. He looks at everyone thinking, "What can this person do for me?"

Peter tries to get the man to see him so they can know each other: "Look at me." The beggar raises his eyes and studies Peter, wondering: "What can I get out of him?" Peter wonders, "How can I help him?" A person wanting to take meets one willing to share. Peter says, "I have no silver or gold; but I give you what I have."

That's different! The beggar is used to people treating him as a beggar and going on in to worship God. But Peter looks into his face and offers what he has. The man realizes he cares. True, Peter doesn't know him, may not even like the look of him, but that's got little to do with it. Caring is a matter of will, not feelings.

So Peter takes his hand. That seems important. Jesus thought so. To convey that he cared, Jesus had to touch the leper, anoint the blind man's eyes. Perhaps our touch speaks where our words can't. When I'm privileged to perform a baptism or a wedding and I touch the baby's head or join the couple's hands in mine, I often think it's a living sign of God's grace flowing. And it does flow, of course.

So Peter grasps the man's hand, and heals him.

What do we moderns think of Christian healing? "Faith healers" have so distorted it by exploitation and superstition that the question is full of confusion. Here's a matter of vital significance both for our personal lives and for humanity's future. The New Testament is filled with potential for spiritual healing. But around us appear con artists, manipulating the naive with stage magic. It's all bewildering and controversial.

But there's an approach to healing that's getting a fresh rehearing nowadays that may help us. "Holism" understands that we are more than a body, we're whole human beings. A patient is not just a sick body, but a sick person, with a body, mind, soul, emotions, family. When your body is diseased, it may partly be because one of those aspects of your life is dis-eased. Your body's illness may not be your basic problem, but a symptom of it, a warning signal that something is wrong with you as a person.

The holistic approach widens the possibilities of healing. I believe that the Holy Spirit works in the deep reaches of our human spirit. Just before we left England, I was asked to preach at a little church in Redruth. After the last hymn, I was about to say the Benediction when a small lady in the third pew said, "Please help me?" She held up her arms. They were covered with thick, red scabs, cracked and bleeding. "I'm like this over all my body. They've done all they can for me. I haven't slept for weeks. I'm going mad with it. Please help me?" She sat down, her face in her blistered hands. I didn't know what to do. There was silence. Like me, the congregation felt lost. Then a man at the back whose head was bowed began a prayer for her. It was a simple prayer. It drew us around that lady in love, and helped us lift her in that love. When he'd finished it was as if everything was drained from him. Then someone else prayed. And someone else...five or six of the congregation, struggling. At last, we went home.

I didn't go to my own church the following Sunday, but back to Redruth. The lady was clean and happy! She'd slept through the night last Sunday. Two friends visited her Monday morning. Healing began. Could it be that her form of dermatitis had its roots in her loneliness?

The congregation, forced by her desperation, had taken themselves seriously as the Body of Christ, and as a channel of God's healing love. They put their arms around her and helped her back to health. Grace flows, believed wise St. Thomas Aquinas, from the soul to the body. Doesn't this understanding enable us personally to respond with hope to spiritual healing?

God's Spirit works in our spirit for calmness and reconciliation. One of my personal saints, Dr. David Shipley, a wise Wesleyan theologian, became terminally ill. His doctor gave him up. So David asked his Administrative Board to pray with him and lay their hands on his head. Timidly, but with love, they did. I wish I'd been part of that group. He recovered. Who knows what the Spirit of God can do?

Is it possible, in the Age of the Spirit that a sick person or someone blind or lame, seeking physical help, can receive it by spiritual healing? That the physical and spiritual intersect?

And of course, there's a more endemic, universal human question that effects us all. Each of us has our own blindness of heart or disability of will or sickness of mind. In the beautiful race through life God offers, some of us limp defectively. We all need healing.

It can happen at both levels when a person responds to God's Spirit of health, as it comes in those moments of grace which occur in one's life; living in Christ shapes like a cross. In the passage from Acts, Peter is letting Christ's Spirit flow through him. As he stretches his arms wide to serve the beggar, he knows the depth of God's love. He shows us that even this love, if it's just an emotion, just a general warm glow for one's fellows, even for the disadvantaged at the door, is useless unless it is directed into action. Love is no good if left as a fuzzy in the heart. Feeling compassion passively is easy and wasted. People of faith are those who have in their hearts the impelling need to act out of God's love. Our inner call to care must be put to work in our churches, in our homes, in our decisions, in the company we keep, in our recreations. For us, love must be evidently and effectively at work in our work.

So Peter grasps the beggar by the hand and pulls him to his feet. That's love in action, risking to act. God's love gets down from the heart into the fingers. Our fingers start to dare, to work, serve, get dirty, get crushed, bleed.

Now come to the height of it, to the lifting life. Even the deeds of love are not enough. Peter opens us to the fullest empowerment of the Spirit. What will change things for church, family, world are the deeds of love which spring to life by believing that in Christ, they will work. Not just deeds of love, then. The Kiwanis and the Boy Scouts do those — and bless them for it. But being empowered by God's Spirit to do deeds of love that are on fire with faith, that's the difference! "In the name of Jesus Christ of Nazareth, walk," Peter says, drawing the man to his feet. He will walk! And the man knows it, too. He gets it through Peter!

Think what it does for the beggar to feel Peter's faith-filled hand, the lifting love of his spirit! It changes his whole way of thinking about himself and his future, as his body comes alive to love. "Immediately, his feet and ankles were made strong. Leaping up, he stood and walked, and entered the temple with them, walking and leaping and praising God." What a wonderful sentence! The most exciting in the scriptures! What a future it opens!

Wouldn't you like to have been in that House of God that day? "He entered the temple with them, walking and leaping and praising God!" Surely there would surge in every worshipper the great empowering hope, "If God's Spirit can do it in that beggar, he can do it in me!" We believe the Spirit is a healing agency, both for ruined or unfulfilled individuals and for our disordered and pain-filled society.

We know the cure is here, and we know how it works. We believe it can give us life, renewal, total resuscitation. All we need is to take it into our bloodstream. And we know what happens: we leap, and walk, and praise God!

For God's Spirit not only can do it in this man: he can do it in us! And God not only can do it through Peter, he can do it through us! This is spiritual life at its truest, its best, its most practical. When we take our faith as something real and life-changing, and let God's Spirit work through us, loving, active, and assured, all things are possible.

There are no exceptions. He can straighten our twisted commitments, clear our hindered sight, and heal us every one. We are then sent out, as healers ourselves, to compassionate deeds of affirming, faith-filled service.

Yes!

Chapter 13: The Spirit's Compass-course

Acts 27:13- 25

They weighed anchor and sailed along Crete, close inshore. But soon a tempestuous wind struck down... and when the ship was caught and could not face the wind, we gave way to it and were driven... As we were violently storm-tossed, they began next day to throw the cargo overboard, and when neither sun nor stars appeared for many a day...all hope of our being saved was at last abandoned.

As they had long been without food, Paul then came forward among them and said, "Men, you should have listened to me, and should not have sailed from Crete and incurred this injury and loss. I now bid you take heart; for there will be no loss of life among you, but only of the ship. For this very night there stood by me an angel of the God to whom I belong and whom I worship, and he said, 'Do not be afraid, Paul; you must stand before Caesar! And God has granted you all those who sail with you.' So take heart, men, for I have faith in God, that it will be exactly as I have been told."

This book, you may recall, I offered as a vessel which takes us out into the deep things of God to discover who we are and what our task is. The metaphor implies a voyage. A voyage implies a charted course, a planned destination. That fits a book, or a voyage of faith. But what of the voyage of life? Does your future have a charted course and planned destination? What will you be doing ten years from now? Is life a matter of chance, of uncharted rocks and wrecks, uncontrollable storms, unpredictable lightning strikes, fogs? Or will God's Spirit somehow shape how the rest of your life turns out?

An eminent Biblical scholar and good friend, Everett Tilson, wrote a book titled *Decision for Destiny*. Why does a faithful Christian write a book on destiny? The word isn't even in the Bible. Destiny has more to do with fate than with faith. If your future is destined, what point is there trying to decide it. Is linking "decision" with "destiny" a silly or a profound paradox?

If our "destiny" is God's will for us, it would be joyous and enabling for us as a Servant Church to know that. God's Spirit would guide our ministry. We could plan how to help people, with no doubts, only the confidence that a caring God will be with us in our service. On the other hand, history shows that when religious people have believed God had a destiny for them, often they felt justified in using any means to achieve it. Recall the Inquisition, Christian slavers, the Empire builders with their "white man's burden," the settlers of the American West with their "Manifest Destiny," S.S. troops of the Holocaust with *Gott mit uns* (God with us) on their belt buckles, and the tragic souls at Jonesville, Waco and Heaven's Gate.

All of us are educated and encultured scientifically. Some of us feel awkward thinking of a Holy Spirit acting in our lives. We are uneasy, too, about Biblical accounts which are based on it. In our opening scripture, Paul was sure he knew God's will because he'd heard a voice in the dark announcing it. If that happened to us, mightn't we suspect a nightmare rather than an angel? Or if we are open to a supernatural explanation, we might equally take it as the voice of a devil.

Earlier we saw the need to check "God's will" by some hard tests. By the Scriptural test of compassion, and by tradition, reason, and our own experience. There are still questions. Does God really bother to inject his will for us even into the minute details of our every day? Or is it only in the big events we can expect interference? Is God acting in everyone's life?

Yet surely in the Age of the Spirit, people of faith should be open to and recognize the Spirit's guidance. I propose three witnesses who will claim that this is so. And in that these soundings have found true Psalm 107's "They that go down to the sea in ships...these see the works of the Lord." Two of the three witnesses tell sea-tales. The first is myself, and a voyage on which the Spirit of God was the compass and set the course. The second is St. Paul, and a voyage which had to do with convicts and a storm, cowardly sailors and a wreck, snake-bite and superstition, a prison cell that became a church, a fire that burned a civilization, and a Spirit who navigated Paul's life (Acts 27). The third is a revered landlubber.

I'll go first.

I was Captain of His Majesty's Ship *Switha*. It was October, 1950. We shipfitters had undergone extensive dockyard repairs and were now doing sea trials, heading up the Channel for Portsmouth. But there were problems. The shipfitters had bungled our magnetic compass. Our radio could receive but not transmit. Still, the weather was fair and we knew the landmarks up the Channel. So orders were to keep going, testing everything. But suddenly at sundown came a thick fog — and instant difficulty. With our only navigational instrument useless, and no means of telling anyone, danger now lay ahead. Between us and Portsmouth was the Isle of Wight, steep-cliffed and deadly. Nearest us were the sharp pillars of rock called "The Needles," the graveyard of innumerable ships over the centuries.

The fog was a dirty great pillow, suffocating us. Tiny whitecaps on the waves, port and starboard, were all we could steer by. I reduced speed, hoped the fog would lift, concentrated on chart work, and felt a tentative way though the gray, silent, cotton-ball night. At midnight I turned 180 degrees. I hoped! Steering by white caps lit feebly by porthole lights doesn't really count as technological navigation. More hours of groping forward, strict chart work, everyone awake, eyes peeled. At 4 a.m. we turned again, back to presumed Northeast.

By now I was worried sick. The crew, entitled like all Royal Navy crews to a nonchalant Captain, were getting just that. Inside, I was a mess.

Morning came, one could just tell through the woolly gloom. I decided, enough blundering about: we'll find the Isle of Wight. We must locate an anchorage, out of the sea lanes, and in water shallow enough for the anchor to reach bottom and there wait until the fog lifted.

Here was the plan. We would edge forward to where my best calculations showed there should be a bay. Stop engines. Have a sailor on the bow take soundings with a lead-line. I'd boom out the ship's siren. Any cliff ahead would bounce an echo back, and I'd measure the distance based on the constant speed of sound at 1,100 feet per second. Knowing depth and distance should help fix our position.

So we began this strange routine. Calculate carefully on the chart. Grope forward. "Stop Engines!" Splash of the lead-line. Sound the hooter: "Whoooooo!" Wait. Then, the seaman's call from the misty bow, "No bottom, sir!" Too deep to anchor. Wait. ...No echo.

Slow ahead again. Where are the Needles? THERE? "Stop Engines!" Soundings, hooter..."No bottom, sir!" No echo. All that dark, gray second day, nothing. Royal Navy face strenuously casual, Don Webb stomach churning, I felt this way and that through the fog. The crew, cheerful and efficient, kept bringing me sweet coffee and sandwiches of french fries in hot bread. I'd been without sleep over 36 hours and faced more. Oh God!

That expletive opened up another option. If there is a God, now was his chance to prove it. Religion is rarely the main thing on a young sailor's mind, but I was desperate. So, new plan. Inch forward, stop engines, make soundings, sound hooter, and *pray*! Might work? Off we go then.

Creep ahead, gently now. Stop engines. Soundings, hooter, pray. "This is very embarrassing, Lord, as you can see better than I can, probably! A five-second echo would be nice, O Lord. Er, amen." Nothing. Try again. Stop engines, soundings, hooter, pray. Still nothing. All though that terrible second night, the tired voice of the leadsman, silence from the fog, and utter silence from above. The night was very long.

Then on the third morning everything happened at once. "Seven fathoms, sir!" An echo — astern! — to port. A dog barked on the port bow. I circled to starboard in case it was someone's front lawn, anchored, and stumbled below to sleep.

Hours later the steward brought tea and a hearty "Nice afternoon, sir! Sun's out!" On deck, I found we'd anchored in the Isle of Wight's popular north coast resort, Bembridge Bay. Off the port bow was a pier, on which the dog had barked and where now two girls were chatting up my sailors. On the port quarter, we'd passed the jagged rocks of a cliff by about 20 yards. Aft to starboard, a U.S. Navy submarine was anchored, its crew staring. On the starboard bow was the huge ocean-liner *S.S. Queen Elizabeth* at anchor, eight hotels tall, her passengers waving. I'd threaded, blind, the lethal Needles — which I wouldn't try in broad daylight in a power boat — groped my way clean round the island and anchored on the safe north coast in the middle of four obstacles any one of which could have sunk us. How?

Oh, not I. I knew now who it was brought us through. It was the God in whose hands are the oceans, and all who sail them. Talk about changing one's life! Needing help utterly, I had pleaded for it and received it. I knew now that God does care about us, has a purpose for our lives, and draws us toward it, even through the Needles of our existence.

Ever since that voyage, mornings starts for me with prayer — "deep to deep." Because every day I need help. Sure, this one's going to be different from every other one, its twists and turns and needs, all surprises. But God has a purpose for it, and for each of us in it. So each dawn I kneel, try to be open to the Spirit of God deeply as I know how, try to sense the pull on my life for this one day; and then move into it with every ability and energy and resource I've got.

Of course, one can decide against putting oneself in the flow. We can live our own way, decide against our "destiny." And certainly, if there's any doubt whether a decision is of God, if one iota of it seems not compassionate, then stop, go back, examine it all again, taking as much time as could possibly be needed for those hard tests; and only when lovingly confident it's indeed of God, then move into it with all eight cylinders. Whether it succeeds or not is up to God. All I have to do is all I can. That's life in the Spirit.

So I accept the confidence of Paul in Acts 27. Having been long in the faith, he felt he could truly sense the guidance of God. I turn to the account with eager anticipation.

Paul had been chained two years in the steaming darkness of Caesarea prison. He looked an old man with his shaggy white hair, lined face and stooped shoulders. But a brightness in his eyes and his chafing at his chains revealed a young man, determined to get out. All his difficulties and rescues had by now convinced him that God had a purpose for his life, and for every life. So he had better get on with God's business.

An idea came to him. It would kill him, eventually and it would change world history. For months, he had been denied a hearing. Then he learned they were going to grant him one, with good chance of release. So Paul demanded his right as a Roman citizen to have his case heard by Caesar himself in Rome. A mad request, with liberty so possible? But he now had an idea what God's plan was. He was to witness in Rome! Jerusalem, the center of religion, had heard the voice of Christ. Athens, the city of learning, had also heard it. Now Rome, city of power, center of empire, crossroads of the world's kingdoms, must hear it — and from his lips! That's why he claimed a Roman's right to be tried in Rome. And that's why we find him, as our sea saga begins, with other prisoners sailing under heavy guard for Crete.

With the chained prisoners battened down below, the ship runs into violent northerly gales, is turned round and sent rushing with tearing canvas toward the dreaded sandbars of the North Africa coast. For ten days it's driven by wind and furious mountains of water, all cargo and spare fittings jettisoned, only the prisoners left to throw overboard. They'll be next.

But Paul knows that God rules all life, all nature, and is not going to let him drown in the hull of a sinking ship. Nor the others either, for they must keep handling the ship. So he rouses them: "Don't lose heart! God means me to appear before the Emperor; no one's life will be lost; trust God!" Is it arrogance or assurance in knowing what your life is for?

Nevertheless, the ship is doomed. For two weeks the chaos of water and wind toss it like a breaking toy. On the fourteenth night, south of the Adriatic, it happens. With rocks ahead and the crew trying to escape, Paul takes charge. If they are to survive, every hand will be needed. He makes them take food. The way he does it, it's like communion, and they come from their common meal with determination. The ship crashes to shore, hits a sand bank and immediately starts to break up. The centurion's duty is to kill the prisoners in case any escape. But he's learned what we know now. When a person with Paul's faith places himself in God's hands, there's no stopping him.

It's terrifying, though. Swept overboard off the coast of Malta, plunged in the boiling ocean, rocks all around, one by one, they struggle ashore in the rain and cold, at what's now called "St. Paul's Bay." For three months, they stay there. The impression one gets is that when Paul leaves, the Maltese are happier and better people. This old man with the young eyes leaves a good feeling in their hearts, an awareness of Christ. He never goes back to Malta. Like Paul, often we have just one chance in a place to leave a Christian feeling.

So we come to the end of the story. In heavy chains, the prisoners are taken to the Bay of Naples, then marched the 130 miles down the Appian Way toward Rome. Even from far away, they hear its noise. At last Paul comes to the Imperial City, because God wants him to witness to Christ there.

He never thought he'd come like this, though, in chains. How can one shackled prisoner in a nameless column move the brassy heart of Rome? Yet if God wants him to be a Christ-person in this city of success, and show the way of love, somehow or another he'll get it done!

He's thrown in a dungeon. The law, grinding slow, leaves him there two years. But he doesn't waste a moment now. He turns his prison cell into a center of dynamic Christianity, the small room becoming more influential in world history than Caesar's palace. Jews and Gentiles come to visit him, question, listen and grow. New energy comes to the other exiled Christians. They begin to speak out and live their faith. Every day, all day sometimes, the room is crowded. Fathers bring their sons. Skeptics go in and emerge whole people; spiritual pygmies become giants; cowards come out determined to walk like Christ. Even Paul's sentries have to listen, and since the guard is changed every few hours, they became a congregation. "Put on the armor of God," he tells them, "Wear the belt of truth!"

We're not sure how he died. In a letter to Timothy he hints that his damp cell makes him cold, and asks for the cloak he left in Troas. Tradition has it he was put to death in the Emperor's massacres. Somehow, Rome caught fire, and Nero, who was the kind of man who would murder his own mother, and did, blamed the Christians. He began their extermination. Maybe Paul died with them.

But we need not mourn for Paul. It would be glorious to live like him. It was the kind of glory that paled even the flames of Rome. The heat of that capital of self left its civilization charred and blackened. But the fire in Paul's eyes, the fire in his faith, lit a message in the sky I can read from here, and you can read from where you are. There's a good course set for us by God's Spirit.

So I come to my third witness. As I've mentioned, it's been my privilege these past months as I've sailed this voyage to empowered service, to have beside me on the desk the New Testament of a truly empowered servant, Ballington Booth. It's become a kind of symbol for me: of those incredible early days of "V of A," and of its valiant faithful leaders. And what a primary resource it's been. Though only when absolutely necessary have I handled it, and turned gently the delicate pages. Ballington often underlined texts vital to him, and a few times wrote a comment alongside in the margin. Mostly, he would carefully insert sheets of blank paper between the New Testament pages, and in a lovely cursive script, in ink — he must have used a fine nib — wrote his notes for sermons he would preach on the adjacent Scriptures.

Often, I've been moved by what he believed and wrote. Imagine my excitement, and complete absorption, at following him as he struggled to respond to God's Word. It's as if I was able to hear what he preached. What he preached helped gather a group of men and women as a Servant Church.

So as I came to this last exploration of God's providence, I obviously hoped that Ballington Booth, too, had found in the Word this same resource both for his own life and the future of the church called Volunteers of America. And the evidence is radiant! From his first sermon to his last, he is sure God has a purpose and plan for the servant life Ballington both chose for himself and saw as the crux of our faith. And he trusted God's Spirit to lead us there.

His first sermon is on Matthew 9:36-38. Jesus was so moved by the plight of the multitudes, he asked his disciples to pray that God "will send forth laborers" for the work of compassion so badly needed. Ballington underlines this heavily, surrounding it with a red crayon border, and writes: "The sending forth. Thrust forth — compel — force them to enter fields." The Spirit clearly purposes it, and plays a strong role in enrolling us in it!

On the mustard seed (Mt. 13:31) he notes, "God's dispensations often at variance with man's plans. His Executions often opposite of man's predictions." He assures convicts, "God only can enable you to realize your true reform...if His Spirit sees you're in earnest he will not see you fail." The familiar saying of Ecclesiastes 9:11, "time and chance happen to them all" he uses as a springboard for the affirmation that God gives a second "chance" to all. Life's hardships he sees fitting into the Divine plan: "In the workings of God's providence...He permits difficulties and obstacles" because it brings believers "to really aggressive service!"

A crucial gift Ballington often lifted up is "heart passion." It leads to "courageous action." So in Romans 1:15, Ballington sees Paul's heart-passion so committed that his human ambition becomes "Holy ambition!" That's what leads "God's servants to put their whole heart into their service." There's a text for "V of A!"

And always he kept the balance. God's grace and our effort. Of "Character" he wrote, "there is no substitute for you yourself;" yet "the responsibility is not self-imposed but God-imposed."

I could go on. It was deep in his faith. Consider his last sermon, "Difficulties as Stepping Stones." It lifted up God's providence and ended with the words — what better epitaph could one have! What more could one affirm at the end of one's Book! — "The future can be left without anxiety in the hands of God, if the heart is His possession." Amen, sir!

So, friends, we can sail our voyage of life fearlessly, by God's grace and with his blessing. The secret is to sense, deep within where the Spirit-compass draws, to set course for the future by it. God's Spirit will lead us even through the Needles of our lives. As God's Servant Church, we're part of a good plan and a good purpose. And as we lift our eyes to the horizon, there is ahead God's "Yes!" in the sky!

Chapter 14: The vision fulfilled

Revelation 21:10

And in the Spirit he carried me away to a great, high mountain.

The Bible culminates in visions. Revelation's seventh and final vision ends "in the Spirit he carried me up to a great, high mountain." There follow, coming down from heaven, the sight of the New Jerusalem where human history will conclude, some encouraging exhortations, a benediction that the grace of the Lord Jesus be with all the saints; and the Scriptures conclude.

But is this what we who have hard facts to face, hard work to do, would have hoped of God's final Word? Up to now as we've responded to Scripture, we've experienced profound yet surely practical edification of life's purposes, and the ability to fulfill them. Of what possible help to us or our needy world are visions? How can rapt Revelation empower us to meet today's cries for help? Forget it, then? I recall a monk whose course on it was titled lightly, "Unscrewing the Inscrutable." But better such whimsy than the fanatical literalism of those who recently killed themselves thinking to board a comet to "Heaven's Gate."

I'm a fairly pragmatic man, I think. Like you, I've bumped against life's hard facts and a few hard tasks along the way. But at seventy-odd, I now stand before this text most gratefully. And I invite you to stand with me awhile. I'll also be so bold as to invite you who are not Christian to stand with me awhile, too. I do believe this Scripture may enable a lifting life for all of us.

I'll be very personal about it. In any case, there's no one way, no one church-authorized way, no one academically-approved way, to experience the Book of Revelation. It was written out of urgent need for courage and self-sacrifice in a Church facing persecution. The stress of that terror may account for occasional sentiments which seem irreconcilable with God's love. We understand that. Some is in code, to confuse the persecutors. As it turned out, "the beast" and "Babylon" did fall, "the Lamb" and his cause did stand. In any case, it's a kind of poetry of faith, at best only sensing what's unknowable, hinting at what's inexpressible. Human language breaks down in face of what is here glimpsed. All of which calls for those tough tests we earlier discussed, of reason, the Church's long tradition, our own experience — and of compassion.

But down the years the church has often found it a Word that brought out new courage and self-sacrifice for the needs of the time. So it's out of that hope and our time's urgencies that I approach this vision. For in it is located what both roots us in our heritage and lifts us to our future.

Certainly much of Revelation seems a bequest from our forebears. Over two-thirds of it echo Old Testament verses; and all of it strongly binds to Christ. Reading it brings the sense of belonging to the people of God and the historic faith. Consider our text. "In the Spirit he carried me up to a great, high mountain." The echo is Ezekiel 40: 2: "in the visions of God brought he me into the land of Israel, and set me upon a very high mountain."

So this is the Spirit of God, then, who bears us. The same Spirit who in Genesis 1 moved over the waters, making with his Word the earth and all on it. The same Spirit who spoke to Abraham, Isaac and Jacob, birthing faith; who spoke through the prophets, time and again, undergirding and clarifying it. It's the same Spirit who taught Israel its primary and vital response to God: to care for the *anawim*, "the widows, the orphaned, and the poor."

And it is the same Spirit who was in Jesus. The Spirit of God himself — the Spirit of love, filling Jesus' life and ministry, death and resurrection. The love encompassed all humanity, all life, even the world whom "God so loved he sent his Son." Who taught us, therefore, above all to "be compassionate, as God is compassionate." And it centered especially on the *anawim*, whom Jesus called "the least," and with whom he identified. Our responding love, our enabled lives, must center on our care of the least. Jesus made it the test of our fidelity. Blessed are those who see Christ in the least, and reach out to them in his service. As I stand before the text, it is this Spirit of love who bears me "into the great, high mountain."

Before considering — ascending! — this mountain, I'd like to speak to my friends for whom God-talk and visions are either unimportant or foolish. I commend to them "Pascal's Wager." Blaise Pascal was a Renaissance man of the 17th century, a mathematician, scientist, savant, and believer. His scientific works far outnumber his theological. One experiment led to the invention of the barometer. But he put an interesting argument to friends who were unconvinced that God exists. At the risk of being importunate and idiosyncratic (pleading Luke 11:8 if so) I propose to improve on his argument. What matters is the lifting life.

Pascal argued that our reason cannot determine God's existence or nonexistence. God isn't an object of our knowledge. Science and philosophy can't help us here. It's more like a bet. If you decide to live as if God exists, you have nothing to lose and everything to gain. If you live as if God does not exist, you have everything to lose and nothing to gain. If you bet God exists, and live so, and you "win" (i.e. there is a God), you win everything — an eternity of life and happiness. If you lose, you lose nothing. It's not a game that can be avoided. There's no third possibility. Either God exists, or he does not. Not to bet is to bet that God doesn't exist. So, what is *your* bet?

The very putting of the argument, Pascal believed, and the reasons for betting "Yes," arouse the will to believe. And after the decision "Yes," understanding comes. The decision is a moment of truth. The penny drops. The light dawns. This is "Pascal's Wager."

Implicit in the argument is the fact that our decision to believe, or not, shapes the way we act. Implicit in this book is the fact that if we do believe, then the way we act shapes in a specific way. If we believe God is who Jesus said he is, a God of compassion, we live compassionately. That is, if we bet there is a God, this God is love. So there is required of us primarily and vitally a life of active love — for God, for all his children, and especially for the rejected, the least. Now, indeed, there is everything to gain and nothing to lose! If there is no God, the world has been helped by us; and we may have some satisfaction. But if there is a God — and there is, and he is as Jesus showed him to be — each child of God we have helped, and we who have helped them, find a lifting life!

Which brings us to the mountain, and opens the future. Pause a moment to read the sublime words of this vision's beginning:

> Then I saw a new heaven and a new earth; for the first heaven and the first earth had passed away, and the sea was no more. And I saw the holy city, new Jerusalem, coming down out of heaven from God, prepared as a bride adorned for her husband; and I heard a great voice from the throne, saying, "Behold, the dwelling of God is with men. He will dwell with them, and they shall be his people, and God himself will be with them; he will wipe away every tear from their eyes, and death shall be no more, neither shall there be mourning nor crying nor pain any more, for the former things have passed away.

What a context in which to receive the future! Suspend for a moment today's hard tasks and hard facts. Sense the Eternal, undergirding this language of poetry and vision, lifting us forward. "The Spirit carried me away to a great, high mountain."

What is this high mountain? Could it be the mountain of faith that has drawn God's people from the beginning? Where Noah's imperiled bark came to safety (Gen. 8:4). Where Abraham and son Isaac heard the angel's life-saving voice (Gen. 22:12). Where Moses received the commandments, on "the mountain of God" (Exodus 3). Where Israel acknowledged their Lord and praised him "on thine own mountain" which "thou hast made for thy abode"(Exodus 15:17). It was on "the mountain of the house of the Lord" that Isaiah received God's promise that when at last, in his love, our world is remade:

> He shall judge between the nations, and shall decide for many peoples; and they shall beat their swords into ploughshares, and their spears into pruning hooks; nation shall not lift up sword against nation, neither shall they learn war any more (Isaiah 2:2).

> They shall not hurt or destroy in all my holy mountain, the wolf shall dwell with the lamb, and the leopard shall lie down with the kid, and the calf and the lion and the fatling together...for the earth shall be full of the knowledge of the Lord as the waters cover the sea. (Isaiah 11:9, ff).

This is the mountain of God's love the Spirit bears us to.

For me, the path up the mountain has been Jesus' Way. My parents and culture raised me so, teaching me to trust Jesus. Since then, I've found it so for myself, much blessed, thanking God. I want to follow utterly the Lord who leads me up the path of the mountain of faith to the God of love.

I have Baptist friends who perceive their path as the sure path — but different from mine. Bless them. I have Lutheran colleagues and Catholic: bless them. We've a daughter in the Reformed Church, a Unitarian son, to both of whom theirs is the sure path: bless them. I witness to my faith gladly, for to me everything depends on it. But I'm not an ultimate authority. I don't know all about God, or all the ways up his holy mountain. Who does? Even Paul admitted, "all that I know is hazy and blurred."

I do believe that as we each climb toward our loving God he sees us, all his children, struggling by our different paths. I believe God wants us to help each other up, bring to the common climb our commitment and compassion. Is this untrue to the thrust of Revelation, which seems so stridently "Christian?" I deeply believe it is not. If this is God's Word, it speaks to us as much as to the first century church. They faced awful persecution and were in danger of apostasy. They needed courage and self-sacrifice, and found them here. The church in our day faces not persecution, but the danger of being irrelevant to God. Our need is for another kind of courage and self-sacrifice.

You recall the account of the little girl back in the hills whose mother died when she was eight? She'd struggled to exhaustion caring for her young siblings, and at 11, dying of tuberculosis, worried that she hadn't taken the children to worship each Sunday. "When I meet our Father, what can I tell him?" Her neighbor took the little callused hands and said, "I shouldn't tell him anything, dear. Just show him your hands."

Did you assume that was a little Christian girl from the hills of Tennessee, perhaps? But if she were a Jewish girl from the Golan Heights, or a Buddhist girl from the Himalayas, will God not take her hands in his and love her? Of course. My Jewish colleagues believe deeply they're on the mountain; I surely won't argue. Nor with Muslim colleagues. Nor do we have to harm each other. We can be grateful that though we're on different paths, we're all on the mountain! And it's God's mountain. The truth is, "he who loves is born of God, and knows God" (1 John 4:7).

And there's one more hope I have of life on the mountain of faith. One day, all people will know God's unbounded love. We will all not only be God's people, but will rejoice to be so. Back in the beginning, Isaiah believed that one day "all nations shall flow" to "the mountain of the house of the Lord" (Isaiah 2:2). Because of my upbringing, I see that hope realized in Jesus of Nazareth. But not in an exclusive way. Jesus was filled with God's love, totally transparent to it, letting it shine and work through all he was and all he did, unimpeded. The first and only one in all human history, I believe, who was all God's love. What he wanted above all was that all should accept this love of God, poured out graciously on all. And live in it. So he says, *"I, if I be lifted up*, will draw all men unto me." To the love. To the acts of love. To God's love. All people!

In this love, hear Jesus' dying words across the pain-filled air to the frightened thief, "Today, you will be with me in Paradise." Today. A thief. I accept that. For myself, too, though my sins are not his. I accept the Lord's Word in 1 Timothy, "God wills that all should be saved, and come to a knowledge of the truth." I accept the Lord's Word in Titus, "For the grace of God hath appeared, bringing salvation to all."

God is love. I cannot let that truth go for any theology. When one sees him face to face, whatever one has done, believed or not believed, the sight of him will kindle at least the beginnings of understanding, at least the start of response — and for many of us, perhaps, the first yearnings for pardon. Which will not be denied, finally. For he loves us. God's ultimate purpose is not defeat — as it would be, if the overwhelming number of his children were excluded. His purpose for all is reconciliation and abundant life. No one knows how and when all of us will one day be drawn to him, but I do believe it. For God loves us all. That's the basic truth about life. That is how God is.

There's an old legend that when the end comes, one day, the disciples will again be sitting with Christ at the Table: waiting to continue the supper. For there is one place vacant. The door opens, and from the night outside comes Judas. Our Lord goes to meet him; puts his arm round his shoulder, and returns the kiss given him by Judas long ago. Then Jesus says, "We have waited for you, friend," and leads him to his place, beside him. On that day, all will be loved ones. And will know it gratefully.

So, friends in the Volunteers of America, may this inheritance lift us forward into our second century and beyond. Who is of God? "Everyone who loves is born of God," believed the founders, who respected all races and religions, and saw themselves as their handmaid and auxiliary. Who are faithful? They who love and feed the hungry, love and clothe the naked, love and visit the convicts. People of different ethnicity or belief, as we are fellow seekers of truth and fellow servants in the love of the God who is Father of us all, we are on the mountain! May there come — in our time! — that beautiful reality of whole life in which the wolf may dwell with the lamb, the leopard with the kid, the calf with the lion, and all human beings, children of God, together in love, in a lifting life that's eternal.

Epilogue: By the light of a good sunset

Allow me one final sounding of the "works of the Lord, and his wonders in the deep." Here we plumb the best and deepest truth of life and servanthood. To approach it, I will share my last experience as a sailor.

We'd just had our third child, Renee and I. We named him Christopher. I still commanded *Switha*, and at 27, I was fairly young. But it seemed time to resign and be a proper father and husband. So I did. Then King George VI died. Elizabeth was to be Queen, and my final weeks were filled with the glorious events of her crowning. The Royal Navy is at the heart of British history, so a high point of a monarch's coronation is the "Review of the Fleet" at Spithead.

Switha was anchored in the front line, and it was all unforgettably splendid: panoply, pomp, and proper pride. Guest warships of many nations joined our assembled fleets. Vessels by the hundred dressed overall, flags by day and myriad lights by night. Talk about majesty! Sailors from all over the world visited each other, swapping tall tales and their respective navy's food. Bands played on quarter-decks. And the Queen in the royal yacht *Britannia* inspected us.

For the final night was planned history's biggest fireworks display. Each ship had been given barrelsful of rockets, whiz-bangs and star shell; on a signal at sundown, we were to detonate the lot. I regret to report, *Switha* did not. The crew persuaded me that ours wouldn't be missed. And they weren't. For hours, the Portsmouth night sky exploded. The fact was, the crew had plans for ours. Next week would be my last with these shipmates; we had grown close, and they wanted to say "God speed" with cheerful bangs of our own. It seemed reasonable. Her Majesty didn't miss a single blast. In fact, she even gave me a medal.

And we had one more treat to come. The Queen asked each ship to select a British port to visit on her behalf, and take royal greetings to her seafaring people. My parents lived in lovely Torbay, in Devonshire, and expected me to choose it. They could come aboard as honored guests. But Torbay is far too lovely. Senior warships would be there by the dozen, and we'd be lost in the brass. No, I knew that coast, and chose instead Salcombe, difficult of access up a kind of narrow fjord, where one ship fills the anchorage. What's more, outside its entrance is a sandbar which big ships can't get over. Even *Switha* could get across only at high tide and with a pilot. In Salcombe, we'd be Her Majesty's sole representative.

This was our last deep-water voyage together, and we made it as much fun as the Queen's Regulations and Admiralty Instructions would allow. Salcombe came in sight. The pilot boarded, guided us over the sandbar and up the fjord; and we anchored. What a week. Now, we used the whiz-bangs! We gave everything we had — fireworks, good hearts, joyous spirits, and hilarious hospitality. They gave us the same! Mom and Dad came overland for a great reunion. Then I left the Navy for a new and even better life.

Stay with me, now: it may not be irrelevant.

For we're to consider that one "deep" ahead of us that for many is most fearful: the event in our voyage of life we call death. Be assured, friend, even in that fathomless trough — especially there — grace enfolds us. The promise of God's loving presence at death is throughout his Word. Before me is Ballington Booth's Psalm 23, heavily underlined: "Yea, though I walk through the valley of the shadow of death, I will fear no evil; for thou art with me." Turning the pages, I see his underlinings of almost every grace-filled assurance of Jesus whose resurrection, he wrote in his fine hand, "is the grand culmination of a life lived for others." Ballington then writes, because he too wanted to be a servant, "Send me!" He underscored "I will never leave thee nor forsake thee" (Heb. 13:6); "Lo, I am with you always, even to the end of the world" (Mt. 28:20), and alongside it, repeated in his own hand, "Listen! Lo, I am with you even...etc. Mt. 28:20." And we've read his moving and relevant "last" words: "The future can be left without anxiety in the hands of God, if the heart is His possession." Ballington

Booth had no doubt that God's grace is forever with us, and goes ahead of us.

I must tell you of my father's death. He fell terminally ill at home in Torbay a few years after Mom died. As he began to sink, my sister Phyllis, who was his dear guardian angel, sent for me from the States. The moment we were all together he revived. We had joyous days and nights by his bed. Though he was dying, he put on a superb effort to be our Dad at his best. He was cheerful, funny and strong.

After two weeks of the deepest love we had ever known, I was called back to the States. We said a love-filled "See you soon," thinking we would. But when I reached home, Phyll telephoned. He had slipped away. Around two a.m. he had called out for her and Elwyn, her husband and his boon companion, and asked them to say the Lord's Prayer with him, one on either side holding his hands. The three said it together, and he died. Oh, those last hours were much confused in Dad's much-medicated mind. But there was that one moment of clarity, one realization of grace. He was prepared. It had made all the difference both to his living and his dying. I've no doubt whatever, friends. God's affirmation also — especially! — enfolds that part of our voyage we call death.

Stay with me one more moment.

Think about our own preparations, yours and mine. We ought to make some. To die is the one thing we all do, sometime. In our love for each other, in God's grace, we should share anything helpful, as we each prepare.

I've written a letter — to my "executrix!" That's a fancy name for the dear girl who will probably have the task of caring for these things. I'd like to share it. It may help you, too. It's written out of gratitude for the best and deepest truth of life.

> Dear Executrix,
> When the time comes, it might be useful to have this gathering-up of the things we occasionally talked about.
>
> Such as, if you know before I do I'm going to die, don't keep it

from me; I believe I can manage it, and I may have things to tidy up. If possible, and the hour is reasonable, call our pastor. He will help us both; perhaps he will have communion with us.

Certainly call him when it happens, even if the hour is unreasonable (I'll try to avoid doing it on a Sunday morning). But call him: he will help you be even more aware than you usually are that God's grace is around both of us.

Then, call a funeral director. In a sense, what's done with my body now makes little difference. I've had three or four new ones since the day I was born (each as short as the last, of course!), my body cells all replaced, over and over, not an atom left of the original bawling infant who on May 4, 1926, entered life in that small bedroom in Wales. But I have not changed; the essential Don Webb has stayed in the successive bodies. So it will be: this frame will again die; but I will have been received back by the God who gave me life in the first place.

So, what's done with my old body doesn't matter too much. Of course, since it has been very good to me in life, I would like it treated seemly. They say, a society which doesn't respect the dead won't long respect the living. But don't be over-concerned with it: that would contradict our Easter faith. Rather, let the funeral be a better witness than any sermon I ever preached, to God's grace, and our gratitude — that we shared happiness all these years, and that now, there come together a family facing death, with a tender Savior.

Therefore, let it be in church. Be where we worshipped together, Sunday by Sunday. We were baptized in church; we married in church: so let the funeral, too, be there — among the understood symbols of our faith, where we have known his love so many times.

The question of whether to have the body viewed publicly beforehand, and whether to bring it into church for the service, I'm avoiding. We'd probably both rather not, but many of our friends look for this way of saying farewell. So, I'm going to do what I've done many times: leave the tough questions to you. We've talked about letting the doctors remove any bits they want; and then, cremation: that would be fine. It's not my body, but the Easter faith, that's the center of things.

We're agreed, no lavish flowers: perhaps a wreath in the shape of an anchor, that ancient symbol of the cross, for old times' sake?

Most folk go for brevity in the service: they may be right. But let scriptures be read; testimony to God's loving kindness; a prayer for comfort, and if you wish, of renewed dedication? Let there be music. No tear jerkers, now: let the victory tunes of life be sung.

Be sure of this: as I write this letter, in face of the ancient problem, how to meet death, there's light all around. For, "if we live, we live unto the Lord; if we die, we die unto the Lord; therefore whether we live or die, we are the Lord's."

Grace and love to you always, Don.

About the sea story with which I opened this sounding of our gratitude: if our life's journey (just once more, then the metaphor can rest) is a kind of voyage, you may guess why Tennyson's *Sunset and Evening Star* means much to me. And why the memory of my last joyous sea voyage in Switha, and the pilot's meeting us, stays deep in me? When our earthly vessels head for the harbor on the other side of death, we can affirm the poet's radiant truth:

> *Sunset and evening star, and one clear call for me.*
> *And may there be no moaning of the bar when I put out to sea.*
> *But such a tide as moving, seems asleep:*
> *Too full for sound and foam,*
> *When that which drew from out the boundless deep,*
> *Turns again home.*
> *Twilight, and evening bell; and after that, the dark.*
> *And may there be no sadness of farewell when I embark.*

> *For though from out our bourne of time and place*
> *The flood may bear me far,*
> *I look to see my pilot face to face,*
> *When I have crossed the bar."*

So God's grace to you, now and always. May it bless your life, and empower your compassionate service.

That God will be with us in our dying does make all the difference to our living. It makes life jubilant now! Every time we experience God's love, it lifts our lives. That's what grace does. But the wonder of this "deep" of God's love is that because we're sure of what happens *then*, at our death, we're empowered for the lifting life *now*! The moment you truly know, deep inside, that the Lord will be with you through the valley of shadow, in that moment of realization, your heart lilts now and from here forward! That's grace! We do nothing to merit being drawn into God's arms. Our response is a heart of thanks, a life of ethics, a being of joy and wholeness.

May we live and serve superbly now by the light cast by the good sunset which is the future of us all.

It's a lifting life!